Architectural Guide
Shenzhen

To my husband, Giuseppe, with boundless love.

Architectural Guide
Shenzhen

Domenica Bona

DOM
publishers

Night skyline from Hong Kong

Contents

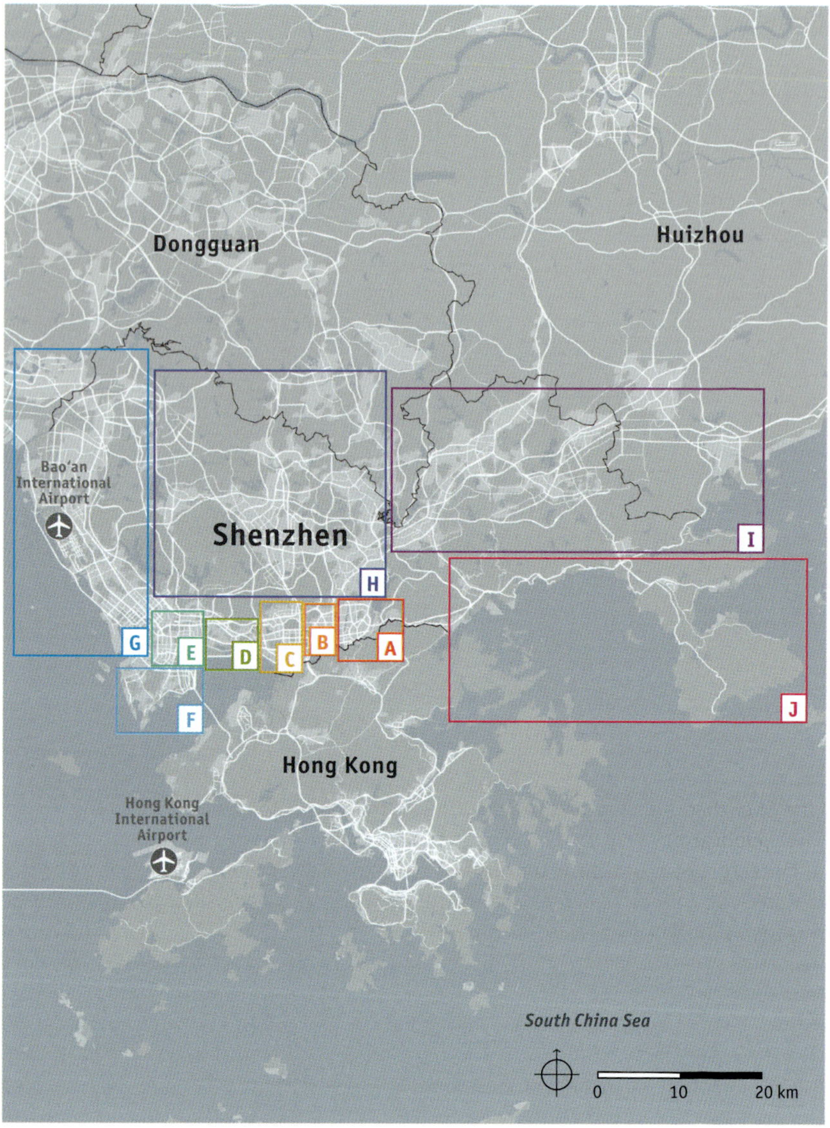

Dongguan

Huizhou

Bao'an
International
Airport

Shenzhen

H

I

G

E D C B A

J

F

Hong Kong

Hong Kong
International
Airport

South China Sea

0   10   20 km

How to use this guide

All projects are marked and numbered on the maps
Where metro information is not listed, it is in the
same location as the previous entry

Project name — **Luohu Art Museum**
Address — Chunfeng Rd. & Nanji Rd., Luohu
Architect — *URBANUS*
Year of completion — 2007

Project number / chapter — 008 A
QR code with geodata

Project name — 罗湖美术馆
Address — 罗湖区春风路和南极路

Metro line/stop — Line 2 Hubei
Walking distance from metro — 湖贝站 400 m

About This Guide

The Shenzhen Architectural Guide is the first publication dedicated to the city's architecture that has been conceived as an atlas. It collects 156 relevant buildings and places that constitute the physical palimpsest of modern China's most famous foundational town.

In general, this guide will introduce the reader to Shenzhen architecture and the broader panorama filled with references to the political history and cultural geography of the city. By photographing the city's state-of-the-art up to 2020, this book frames a sort of *hic et nunc* that will soon be different again. The 10 chapters that compose the book present Shenzhen according to a geographical route, starting from the Sino-British border in Luohu, its inner districts, and then the outer territories. This itinerary follows the timeline of Shenzhen's urbanisation: from the modernism of the *tabula rasa* to the rediscovery of a pre-urban heritage. Every chapter features an essay introducing the peculiarities of the urban context, its history, and its architectural consistency. Each section is accompanied by a map showing the area's cartographic abstraction with relevant toponyms and labels that refer to the pieces of architecture presented.

The selected projects all feature the essential data in both English and Chinese languages, which will allow visitors to easily reach the sites and ask locals about them. These projects are not exhaustive of the city's kaleidoscopic architecture; that said, while visiting these buildings, visitors can quickly stop over plenty of other interesting spots. The order of projects suggests a tour that continues chapter by chapter in a unique sequence. Distances dilate as we leave the Special Economic Zone (chapters A–F) and move across the outer districts (chapters G–J).

Notes for Newcomers

Be ready to walk, take taxis, use the city's efficient public transportation, and, especially in the farthest areas, jump behind a motorbike with an illegal driver who will bargain the fare to bring you to some of the most remote places. It's all fine – just relax and get used to the local habits and tropical weather that will make you sweat most of the time, even when you aren't moving.

Xili Village under demolition, 2010

An Empiric Geography

In 2010, I moved to Shenzhen to study at Shenzhen University College of Architecture and Urban Planning. At that time, few could speak English, even on campus. For me, that experience was a cultural shock that would change my mindset and my future career. I learned Mandarin from my classmates, office colleagues, waiters, and taxi drivers; in fact, I learned a lot about the local culture from them, but not that much about the city itself.

I had been in Shenzhen for a couple of weeks when my urban planning professor brought our class to visit Xili Town, where the Shenzhen Higher Education Mega Centre (see p. 214) was under construction. There, the bus left us on an empty street where bulldozers were busy demolishing what I would later discover were the 'handshake buildings' of Xili urban village. I don't remember any critical opinions from my teacher or Chinese classmates about this common practise to raze and rebuild, making space for new buildings for a better urban environment. Nevertheless, it felt like too much for me to digest at one time. So, I have continued studying Shenzhen's urban evolution over the past decade, from cultivating relationships and research projects, to mapping the urban growth, to analysing the architectural change and dystopic phenomena that define this peculiar cultural geography.

Shenzhen became an obsession, and I am deeply immersed into its nebula of doubts, epiphanies, and topics to disentangle. Above the rest, there's a question that has accompanied my research: Is Shenzhen truly the 'cultural desert' claimed by propaganda? Is it really the product of a post-Mao utopia, or is it something else? This question about the city's 'cultural milieu' began to be answered long before I started to work on this book, after years of visits, discussions, and investigations to understand Shenzhen and its urban history piece by piece. It's possible that the last 10 years have driven Shenzhen to a certain maturity in the way it perceives itself. Indeed, this is a culminating moment in the city's design history, and an excellent time to look back to 40 years of urbanisation and architectural production. In this span of time, buildings, and places, Shenzhen's cultural geography could define its own path before becoming overrun again by the next change.

Sham Chun River

Caiwuwei Village

View of Caiwuwei Village from Diwang Tower (see p. 58)

012 Financial Centre

013 Shenzhen Development Bank

Shenye Centre

Jinshan Mansion

Shennan East Road

The Making of a Dream City

Shenzhen is generally portrayed as a 40-year-old city built on a *tabula rasa* where only 30,000 peasants and fishers lived before the city was founded in 1978. Narrated in these terms, Shenzhen seems like a city without a past, although a millennial history testifies three significant moments in the history of this land of Souther China: the pre-modern rural period, the Maoist collectivisation, and the post-Mao reform booming period.

A Morphological Reading

Shenzhen's morphology recalls the shape of a dragon – a symbol of power, strength, and good luck. Capable of controlling water, typhoons, and floods, the dragon is a spiritual protector of Shenzhen's river valley, opened to the sea and touching the river's flow. At the southern edge of the eastern Pearl River Delta banks, Shenzhen grew at the border with the Hong Kong peninsula, naturally separated by Shenzhen River, which flows into Shenzhen Bay, and famous for its mangrove trees forests. Thus configuring an ideal space for urban development dictated by the natural geography of the place, the tropical weather of southern Guangdong Province enriches the local flora and fauna of abundant vegetation, colourful birds, and a marine landscape that tends to prevail despite the human transformations of the land. The alluvial plain where Shenzhen was settled early on is enclosed by the mountains to the north and the Shenzhen River and South China Sea to the south, and stretched out by the Nantou Peninsula to the west and the Dapeng Peninsula to the very east. The early settlement's location was strategic for attracting Hong Kong's industries and helping them develop a strong, provision-oriented economy here where the land was extensive and accessible.

Nantou Before Shenzhen

Since ancient times, the area has been important for the sea field developed along the coasts. A salt attendant was, indeed, settled in Nantou Peninsula. During the Ming dynasty, the area was identified as Xin'an County and Nantou Walled City (see p. 145) became the county seat. Here, thanks to the Pearl River's deep water in the east and the protected harbours, the county flourished, becoming a convenient access point for merchants

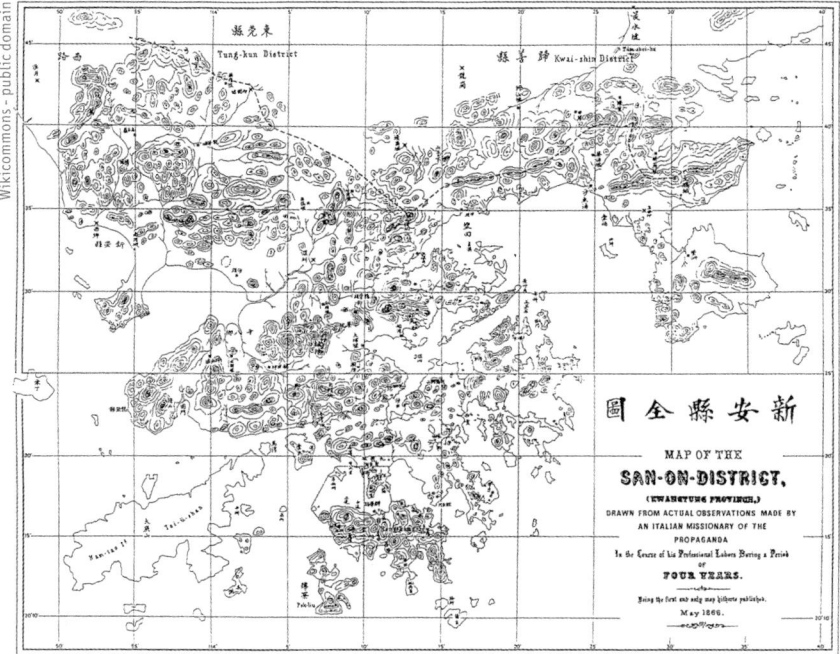

Map of Sanon District (Bao'an County) by the Italian missionary Simeone Volonteri, 1866

and a strategic output for maritime defence. Chronicles, for instance, say that Admiral Zheng He and his fleet stopped in the Chiwan Port and visited Tianhou Temple (see p. 177) during their exploration voyages towards Africa (1405–1433). During the Ming dynasty, a marketplace was settled 40 kilometres east of Nantou. The walled compound had four gates and served the surrounding villages, which could rent a stall on three days of the 10-day cycle. The Hakka villages of the eastern valleys found the Shenzhen market a convenient place to trade their goods, connecting their own culture to the local Cantonese one. With the British colonisation of Hong Kong after the Treaty of Nanjing (1842), the

Ancient map of Nantou Old Town

Shenzhen Reservoir construction site, 1960

Sino-British border was drawn along the Shenzhen River, just south of the Shenzhen marketplace. In 1913, the Kowloon-Canton Railway's construction across the river and the Shenzhen Market station's opening on Chinese soil led to the loss of Nantou's importance in favour of the border area called Luohu.

With the rise of Communism, Xin'an County changed its name to Bao'an County and the region again became crucial for its proximity to the British colony. In 1953, the Bao'an County seat was moved from Nantou Old Town to Caiwuwei in Luohu near the Bamboo Curtain, as the border was called. This decision was the first sign of a political attempt to rebalance Hong Kong's pressure on the land and to better control people's and goods' transit along the border. Moreover, Mao's collectivisation changed the social structure of Bao'an County. The Hakka people were pushed out of their villages in the eastern valleys and transformed into self-sufficient rural communes of local and immigrant peasants producing agricultural products necessary to feed the brigades that were busy in other

People walk through the Luohu Bridge to their hometowns, 1979

Zheng Zhongjian (Shenzhen Evening News)

Friends of the Huang Ho (Shenzhen Evening News)

(q578.com)

Shenzhen street view in the 1980s

productive sectors. The anglers' households were aggregated into brigades and given the land to build dormitories, shared facilities, schools, and fish processing plants on the coast. Along the Sino-British border, new bridges were built along with warehouses and administrative and commercial venues that could take advantage of the flow of goods and people across the border.

It was too early to forecast the upcoming events. Still, by this time it was already clear that proximity to Hong Kong would eventually make Bao'an County a strategic spot for the future destiny of the country's economy and diplomacy in the post-Mao era.

Master Planning an Urban Utopia

The first act of Deng Xiaoping's reform agenda corresponds to the institution of four coastal Special Economic Zones (SEZ) in 1978, among which the most crucial one was Shenzhen. Its proximity to Hong Kong and potentially available land made the state focalise the highest ambitions on what the city could do for the

View of Shennan Road from the Grand Theatre

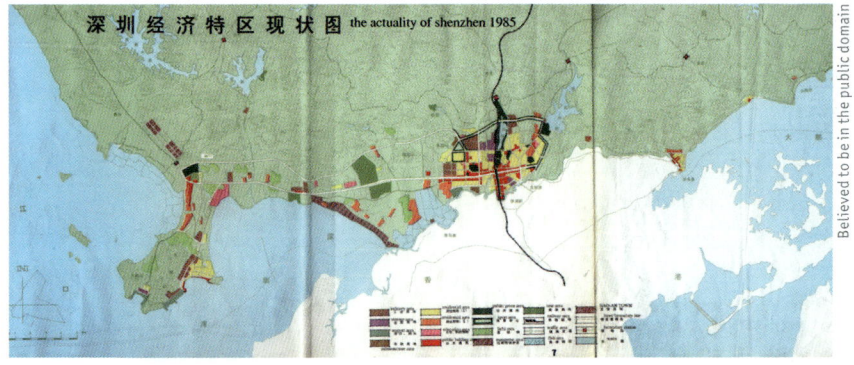

The actual plan of Shenzhen in 1985

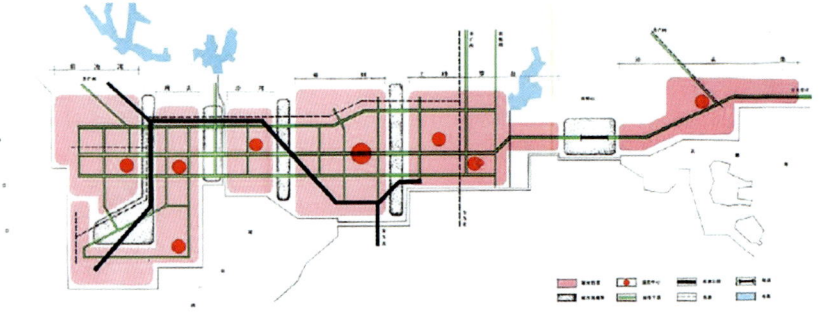

The urban structure and 1986 master plan

The master plan of 1986–1990

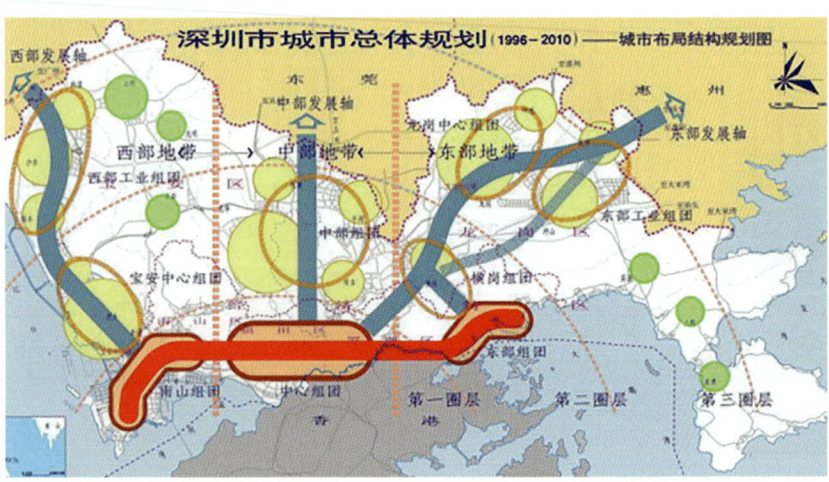

The urban structure and 1996 master plan

national economy and prestige. Immediately, the SEZ border was drawn across the stretched strip of land closed between Hong Kong and the sea at the south and the mountains at the north. Then, in 1979, the Guangdong Provincial Standing Committee elevated the administrative status of Bao'an County to Shenzhen Municipality in order to strengthen governance over its territory and stimulate the city's opening and development.

Starting from scratch had not been an easy job for Shenzhen officers at that time. To create working units capable of managing and realising the urbanisation program, from 1978 to 1982, the Central Government deployed the People's Liberation Army Engineering Corps. The group built the necessary infrastructures and institutional buildings of the newly born city, concentrating their efforts on Luohu and its surroundings. In parallel, under the motto 'Time is Money, Efficiency is Life', the China Merchants Group started to operate in the Shekou area, boosting port activities in a private-public alliance that would soon lead the company to achieve the economic fortune of the SEZ.

The first comprehensive master plan of the Shenzhen Special Economic Zone was drafted in 1982 and aimed to clarify the strategy of future urban development by strengthening the administrative role of Luohu District through its railway station and checkpoint to Hong Kong, locating port facilities along the west river bank in Shekou and the eastern oceanic coast in Yantian, and founding the first export-oriented free zone in Shekou. Here, the state sought to attract Hong Kong's industries and help them develop a robust, export-oriented economy with an extensively free and attractive environment.

In 1986, the second master plan better identified the morphology of the urban settlement. The structure was that of a polycentric linear city, with several cores connected by three east-west road axes and fragmented by 13 north-south primary roads. The linear model represents an attempt to transform Shenzhen's urbanisation into an urban prototype capable of turning the utopian visions of many twentieth-century planners into reality. These planners had been fascinated by the idea of building countless rational, modern, efficient, and democratic cities. Besides the political connotation of the unbuilt prototypes, Shenzhen was planned to become a model or 'dream' city, to echo famous mass cities like Los Angeles.

The primary urban clusters located along the longitudinal axis, from east to west, are: Yantian, Luohu, Futian, Nanshan, and Shekou, the aforementioned place of the earliest marine land reclamation. Each district is separated by green belts and equipped with primary services. Typically, the whole structure follows an exact protocol: The two main clusters of Nanshan and Luohu, located at opposite

坚持党的基本路线一百年不动摇

xiquinhosilva (Flickr)

The Deng Xiaoping billboard near Lychee Park

013 **Shenzhen Development Bank**

014 **Diwang Tower**

015 **KK100 Kingkey Tower**

024 **Hui Hotel**

023 **China Telecom**

Pangling Plaza

Hung Cheong Plaza

004 **Guomao Building**

007 **Golden Business Centre**

A view of Luohu District from Lianhuashan Park

ends of Shennan Avenue – the primary express road spanning east-west – were the first to be built and specialised. Nanshan District was dedicated to industries, universities, and port activities, and Luohu to commercial and managerial activities, as noted by the first Central Business District (CBD) and the railway station. The land in the middle was intended for successive phases of expansion.

Until 1996, urbanisation and economic growth ran so fast that they catalysed an impressive amount of investments, workers, and trades never before experienced in pre-reform China. The construction of infrastructures continued at a fast pace, generating a grid of plots to fulfil according to a modern zoning approach. The unbuilt SEZ areas were then ready to be developed, such as the Futian Central District for which a design competition took place in the same year. The third master plan in 1996 is the basis of Shenzhen's current structure; indeed,

020 SEG Plaza

it is the first that drafts the city's expansion to the northern territories of Bao'an, Longhua, and Longgang beyond the SEZ border. Often called the 'Second Line', it marks an administrative boundary and the social status division of citizenship and ruralship, with the related social issues that these divisions imply. The master plan is one of the first urban-rural plans drawn up in China. On one hand, it extends the infrastructure network to cover Shenzhen's entire administrative area, increasing from the SEZ's 300 square kilometres to a total of 2,000 square kilometres. On the other hand, it defines natural reserve areas subject to restrictions and saved from the soil's impending consumption. Nevertheless, the municipal areas beyond the SEZ became the new land of conquest for industries and real estate. Manufacturers and heavy industries moved in from the SEZ, finding better infrastructure and more available space. New several-million-people-sized

001 Luohu Port Control Point

002 Shenzhen Railway Station

Hong Kong New Territories

Grand Hyatt Shenzhen

Felicity Hotel

The MixC

(zhuanlan.zhihu.com)

Minghua Ship docked along Shekou seafront, 1990s

towns are condensed around pre-existing villages and sprawl into a continuous and undistinguished settlement, framed by the natural morphology.

Enlarge. Make Space. Reclaim the Land.

Urban growth did not just sprawl beyond the 'Second Line' and into the northern districts, but rather, from the beginning, it pushed planners to develop a consistent program of land reclamation so as to produce new space inside the Special Economic Zone. Especially along the Pearl River's west bank and inside the Shenzhen Bay, where the water was not significantly deep, the coastline has shifted several times in the past decades. This has increased the amount of exploitable land for real estate, defining a flat fancy landscape that now mostly replaces the original mangrove trees and oyster cultivation. Reclamation after reclamation, the Nantou Peninsula is undoubtedly the area that has most grown in surface area. On the east side, the Houhai Sub-district lies on reclaimed land, like the One Shenzhen Bay development (see p. 159), the Shenzhen Talent Park waterfront, the Shenzhen Bay Terminal, and the Shenzhen Bay Bridge (see p. 168). In the south, Shekou port has gained enough land to establish a container terminal that competes with the top 10 ports in the world. Here,

He Huangyou

Shenzhen University in Nanshan before the land reclamation on Shenzhen Bay, 1984

NASA

Land reclamation near Nanshan Peninsula as measured by Landsat in 1975

NASA

Land reclamation as measured by Landsat in 1995 – in yellow, the coastline in 1975

Land reclamation as measured by Landsat in 2001 – in yellow, the coastline in 1975

Land reclamation in 2002 – in yellow, the coastline in 1975

the most obvious trace of the reclamation process is the Minghua Ship stranded at Sea World Plaza (see p. 173). To the west, Qianhai Bay has been almost fulfilled, making space for the latest SEZ business district. Going north, the Bao'an coast, primarily used for fish farming, has been converted into a transportation hub featuring an international airport and a vast network of infrastructures connecting the two sides of the Pearl River Delta.

Build. Raze. Rebuild.

In Shenzhen, as one overlooks the urban landscape from the high floor of a skyscraper, the most contrasting sight at first glance is the surgically marked the boundary between Shenzhen and Hong Kong. On one side, dense buildings have eaten as much land as they can. On the other, water ponds and crops remind us of how this entire area was before 1978.

Needless to say, the natural environment is the most evident casualty of urbanisation. About 150 hectares of mangrove forest have vanished, high grounds have been flattened, and an entire ecosystem has been damaged by years of industrialisation. However, a wise ecological agenda has bridged Shenzhen in becoming a low-waste green city capable of inverting its carbon footprint, cleaning up kilometres of polluted waterways, and addressing a sustainable urban culture.

Moreover, land preservation policies introduced in 1996 have secured the unbuilt environment from thoughtless use and total land occupation. However, land-use control has challenged stakeholders in finding other ways to feed the construction industry. If they could not build on every free square metre, they had to find other options, like redeveloping the earliest built fabrics, which were usually in poor conditions, low density, and located in the city's strategical areas.

This modus, while apparently standard, has produced the urban fabric's continuous transformation, making up a large part of the dystopian phenomena afflicting the city. On the one hand, it has contributed to redeveloping the Special Zone's former productive areas that have relocated to the northern districts, making them attractive for the real estate market. On the other hand, the archipelago of informal settlements nestled into formal areas suffers from real estate pressure. Willing to buy the building rights for these plots of land, it has already razed a large amount of the self-built handshake buildings and, as a consequence, massively relocated the low-income communities living there to make space for new gentrification projects. As a matter of fact, the Shekou motto 'Time is Money, Efficiency is Life' is genuinely rooted in Shenzhen's consumption culture that constantly seeks new achievements, far

View of OCT East residential community

View of northern Luohu from Diwang observation deck

View of Huanggang from the top of an apartment block

from producing a static and quiet image of the city and its inhabitants.

Theorising the Shenzhen Speed

Completing the Shenzhen urban agenda required much energy and effort, especially in terms of working hours and the number of workers employed on the construction sites. A non-stop rhythm has characterised its urban growth since the early days of the Special Economic Zone and the speed has been enhanced by employing more workers, introducing work teams, and letting them work longer. At that time, the national media emphasised the 'Shenzhen Speed', so it was called, referring to the incredible ability to build the Guomao Building (see p. 46) at a pace of one storey every three days. Even Deng Xiaoping praised such speed as the fuel of the city's chance to compete with any other global city. This form of exploitation represented the way to gain success. In fact, it became a sign of patriotism, of the individual contribution that each worker could give to the national cause of building an urban utopia.

However, Shenzhen Speed also had other implications. Despite the coin's glorious

(Bigstock)

Residential buildings in Luohu

(q578.com)

Shenzhen street view in the 1980s

fold, workers' living conditions have been challenging as they are far from their families and framed into a brigade lifestyle that recalls the Maoist communal life of some 50 years ago. Without a doubt, the government and stakeholders have taken on a hefty dose of risks in building a metropolis from the ground up. Simultaneously, planners and designers have handled the immense quantity of designs by often applying low-risk formulated plans and, like real estate, employing generic marketing strategies. Architectural recipes – the ready-to-use atlas of plans found on the bookshelves

of architects' offices who are too busy to explore more creative projects – are at the base of the nearly identical commercial buildings, apartments blocks, and neighbourhoods. These works frame the outstanding pieces of architecture that dot Shenzhen and are usually designed *ad hoc* by well known architectural offices from China and abroad.

Dystopic Phenomena of Livability

Despite the original meanings associated with the Shenzhen Speed, more recently, the word 'speed' has come to refer

Friends of the Huang Ho (Shenzhen Evening News)

Guomao Tower and Luohu District overlooking Hong Kong New Territories, 1985

A wet market street in an urban village, 2016

Handshake buildings in Luohu

to the psychological burn out of many Shenzheners who are seeking, one the one hand, their piece of the dream and, on the other, a shared local culture with which they can identify. Over the years, social issues have often been associated with the evolution of Shenzhen's urban space, and most of them find their *raison d'être* in the 'urban villages'. Political rhetoric aside, the urban villages could be described as places where people could change their fates and follow the Shenzhen Dream. Initiated by the former peasants who once belonged to the farming brigades that occupied the land before the foundation of Shenzhen, these hyper-dense informal settlements represent the counterpart to the vast and modern urban fabrics of the formal city.

Shenzhen is called the city of ten thousand villages because of the conspicuous number of informal settlements nestled into the urban fabric of the SEZ, as in the northern districts, where these villages often swallow up traces of the original Cantonese and Hakka dwellings. Since the 1970s, millions of poor immigrants have found low-budget accommodation to rent in one of the many 5-to-7-storey-high blocks with an area of approximately 100 square metres, mostly clad in colourful tiles. The so-called 'handshake buildings' all look the same, and they are built so close to each other that – according to urban myths – people can shake each other's hands from their front windows.

The origin of these buildings is curious, and one should try to imagine that before 1992, farms with stables and small rural buildings were in their place. In the 1980s, when the urban road network started to frame former farms, villagers were soon no longer farming. As a result, they started to build free-standing homes for themselves and some collective rental properties for shops and dormitories. Then, in 1992, a policy limited the villages' land resources inside the SEZ, so villagers began building multistorey buildings occupying the available land and generating a new kind of urban pattern of dense structures often lacking

A construction site replacing part of Gangxia Village (see p. 101), 2013

the basic infrastructures and in poor hygienic conditions. Here, workers could afford simple accommodations and take advantage of a wide range of services and social supports that contributed to making each village into a real community.

Besides the controversial living conditions, the new pattern counterbalances the sense of displacement of such a futuristic and out-of-scale city. Al fresco dining, small convenience shops, and other street activities attract swarms of people all day long to create a vibrant street life that contributes to a positive underground urban culture mixing rural and urban elements and shades from every province of China.

As the urban expansion sprawled outside of the SEZ in 2004, the remaining land under village control and was transferred to the city, which was already conducting a battle to demolish and evict urban villages in order to develop upscale real estate, such as gated communities,

(Bigstock)

malls, and other gentrification projects. In 2018, after countless reactions against the demolition proposals, the government improved its affordable housing program by defining new strategies to upgrade villages and legally frame them into the urban apparatus. Nevertheless, today's urban villages in the SEZ are shadows of what they were 20 years ago, especially the biggest ones, including Caiwuwei in Luohu, Gangxia (see p. 101) in Futian, and Baishizhou (see p. 134) in Nanshan. The villages' destinies are still undetermined, and the controversial relationship between rural and urban is far from being uprooted from the city's DNA. The local government tried to solve this dichotomy in administrative terms but without strategical change in the spatial, social, or cultural folds.

Mapping a Cultural Geography

When Japanese architect Arata Isozaki visited Shenzhen in 2006, at the time of his project for the Shenzhen Library and

Apartment block near Bao'an Stadium (see p. 188)

URBANUS, *tulou* **within urban village, 2008**

Concert Hall (see p. 92), he said that, 'Shenzhen should be the place to show-case Chinese cultural essences. When buildings, culture, and environment are perfectly integrated, Shenzhen should include different cultural elements across the country into its architectures'. Isozaki probably caught the city's essence before others by emphasising the metacultural challenge that such an unconventional city would face.

Shenzhen is known for its cultural melting pot of immigrants coming from all around the country. In addition to this famous side of the story, Shenzhen is also recognised as the meeting point of four peculiar cultures, related to three distinct ethnic groups, each with their habits, ethos, and histories: the Han, representing the national common ground; the Cantonese, an autochthon population of the Lingnan; the Hakka, a rural population migrated from the Yellow River basin under persecutions during the Song and Ming dynasties; and the Overseas Chinese, entrepreneurs who made a fortune abroad before investing back in the motherland. Suppose the Special Zone is the state and Overseas' place, while the north-west territory is that of the Cantonese. In that case, north-east Shenzhen is

where the Hakka people flourished, leaving most traces of their predominancy over the East Guangdong province. Far from combining into new, integrated forms, these four cultures have played distinctive roles in Shenzhen's urban development, and, certainly, their coexistence has given rise to opportunities and conflicts. With the reforms, Shenzhen soon adopted Hong Kong's habits, not just in doing business but also in shaping urban life at the border, giving birth to a fifth new 'cross-border culture', defining the new mass culture of consumption. In the 1980s and still somewhat to this day, Shenzhen became famous for al fresco dining and night markets, mimicking Hong Kong's Temple Street and Ladies Market. Malls and new commodities gave people access to Western-like lifestyles, with Dongmen Street (see p. 48) and Guomao Building (see p. 46) in Luohu appointed as the centres of this booming market culture.

At the beginning of the reform, political ideas were infused with a new Confucianism recalling the Chinese philosophical principles of the Golden Age and the legacy of the literati Mao – concepts that the Shenzhen model should evoke. Somehow, the way the urban landscape was designed evokes a Neo-Maoist arcadia animated by the principle of returning to nature – here in the sense of human nature that can achieve freedom of spirit in harmony with the environment.

In Shenzhen, landscaping aims for perfection, from the thousands of gardens to the smallest flowerbed. This new natural aesthetic symbolically reflects the city's ethos of communal participation in achieving a shared goal. The Shenzhen University Campus (see p. 152) and Lianhuashan Park (see p. 94) are great examples of this symbolical geography of Shenzhen that comprise the so-called five lakes and four oceans from Mao's statement, 'We have come from the five lakes and four oceans to achieve a shared revolutionary goal': East Lake, Shiyan Lake, Silver Lake, Xili Lake, Xiangmi Lake, and Daya Bay, the Big and Little Meisha Beaches, Shekou Bay, and Shenzhen Bay.

Pushing Fame Beyond

Shenzhen put great emphasis on its economic power, innovative culture, and past-less orientation towards the future. Being powerful, green, and sustainable led the city to enter the hall of fame among the world cities. In doing so, high-tech industries, like design,

architecture, and IT contributed to establishing Shenzhen as a research centre and innovation base.

In the architectural and design fields, Shenzhen is famous for hosting the 'Bi-City Biennale of Urbanism/Architecture' with Hong Kong since 2005 and has been one of UNESCO's 'Cities of Design' since 2008. Over the years, the Biennale has provided the opportunity to experiment with and open the debate on urbanisation with the rest of the world, putting the city at the centre of urban discourse and challenging architects and planners to share knowledge and develop a new criticism and creative freedom. URBANUS, the local office of architecture and planning that greatly participated in the city building, is undoubtedly one of the principal advocates of the local urban debate. It spent plenty of energy researching the potentialities behind the urban density, the role of urban villages, and the way to bridge Shenzhen into a sustainable future that does not turn its back to its history. Nevertheless, for Shenzhen, being without a past represented the best slogan that marketers could invent to promote what was to be considered the newest, most innovative, most unseen city in the world. It was perfect for attracting workers, investments, and media in the

A tree-lined yard near Shenzhen University's teaching buildings (see p. 152)

A sidewalk in Longgang

beginning. It continued to work for almost four decades, despite scholars' and academia's first claims that Shenzhen was more than a mythological *tabula rasa* and that its past needed to be investigated. Considering Shenzhen a city without a past was acceptable until the second generation of Shenzheners had grown up enough to feel the need to recognise themselves in the city's past, to know more about the local culture, and to become members of a community rooted in something more profound than a *tabula rasa*. Again, most Shenzheners are immigrants who arrived here in search of fortune. Some of them have chosen not to go back home, giving birth to the second generation of Shenzheners who do not feel the same sense of belonging to their parents' original cultures. In recent years, amid the move from a planned to a market economy, the growing demand

Vendors of a shop near Tianhou Temple (see p. 177)

URBANUS, Baishizhou 5 Village Urban Design, Dencity, 2016

for culture led Shenzhen to again change its clothes rapidly. Thanks to citizens' active participation, cultural festivals sprouted up in many former village communities, especially in Bao'an and Longgang, where Cantonese and Hakka people still live. Temples, as well, saw a new wave of devotion by long-term residents who have contributed to the renovation. Moreover, the local communities' forceful actions have prevented the demolition of a certain amount of villages and historical sites that are now lively cultural centres, like Nantou Old Village (see p. 145) in Nanshan and Fenghuang Village (see p. 194) in Bao'an.

A richly built heritage has emerged all around the city in a short time. Some sites have already been restored by the public and the family clans initially entitled to the site. In some cases, real estate companies have transformed decadent places into commodified touristic attractions, where shopping is housed in old residences surrounded by movie-like scenographies, like in Gangkeng Ancient

Hakka Town (see p. 212) in Longhua district. Nevertheless, what before was hidden and unseen, today is at the centre of a new cultural debate that, far from being underground, the government is encouraging. Indeed, because the economy was the early key to levelling up Shenzhen in the rank of cities, today culture is the city's new tool to upgrade its status and become attractive for more than just business.

Stakeholders are considering the alternatives to demolishing older sites in order to make space for the umpteenth land speculation. This does not mean the end of contradictions, but Shenzhen is undoubtedly maturing and, with this maturity, it must grapple with how things happen within its boundaries. Upgrading but not demolishing has recently become a new mantra that could help, on the one hand, to maintain the peculiar balance between dichotomies like rural and urban, formal and informal, traditionalist and innovative, and, on the other hand, in preserving the heterogeneity and authentic character of this city rooted in such chasms.

SEZ East
Luohu, Guomao, Caiwuwei, Cuizhu

Luohu border in 1964 (top) and 2000 (bottom)

The Making of the One Night City

Eighteen kilometres of alluvial land connects the former British colony of Hong Kong to Mainland China from south to north and Mirs Bay to Shenzhen Bay from east to west. The Sham Chun River physically marks the so-called 'Bamboo Curtain' while the Luohu Bridge represented the only link on earth between the two countries for more than a century. The opening of the first station on the Chinese side the Kowloon-Canton Railway (KCR) and the transfer of the Bao'an County's administrative centre to Caiwuwei in 1953 would soon activate a radical transformation of Luohu. Under Mao, small extant villages near the border were converted into peasant and fisher brigades, and agricultural processing facilities were built on the side to boost exports to Hong Kong. In 1980, the need to develop the Special Economic Zone from scratch allowed the government to start constructing a new urban utopia in Luohu through the hands of the People's Liberation Army Engineering Corps.

Little evidence of the past remains apart from the urban villages and the spirit of glorious market places such as Dongmen Market Street (see p. 48), some repurposed manufactures like the YUE Art Gallery (see p. 52), and, without a doubt, the rural landscape of rice paddies behind the border. The rest tells the story of the Reform and Opening period when Luohu was considered the 'one night city' of tomorrow with the Guomao Building (see p. 46) and its revolving restaurant, the Luohu Shopping Mall facing the Railway Station (see p. 44), and Lychee Park with the famous Deng Xiaoping billboard right in front of the early Shenzhen business district which was designed as a financial acropolis, framed by the futuristic Diwang Tower (see p. 58) and Shenzhen Development Bank (see p. 56).

Indeed, Luohu embodies all of the early values from the first generation of Shenzhen's market culture, based on consumption and Westernised habits, mixed with the rural traditions conserved by people in their daily lives. The post-modernist appearance of Luohu architecture fits the ambivalence of Shenzhen's early days perfectly because it combines international language, national instances, proto-capitalistic values, a still-human scale, futuristic visions, political utopias, and social dystopias.

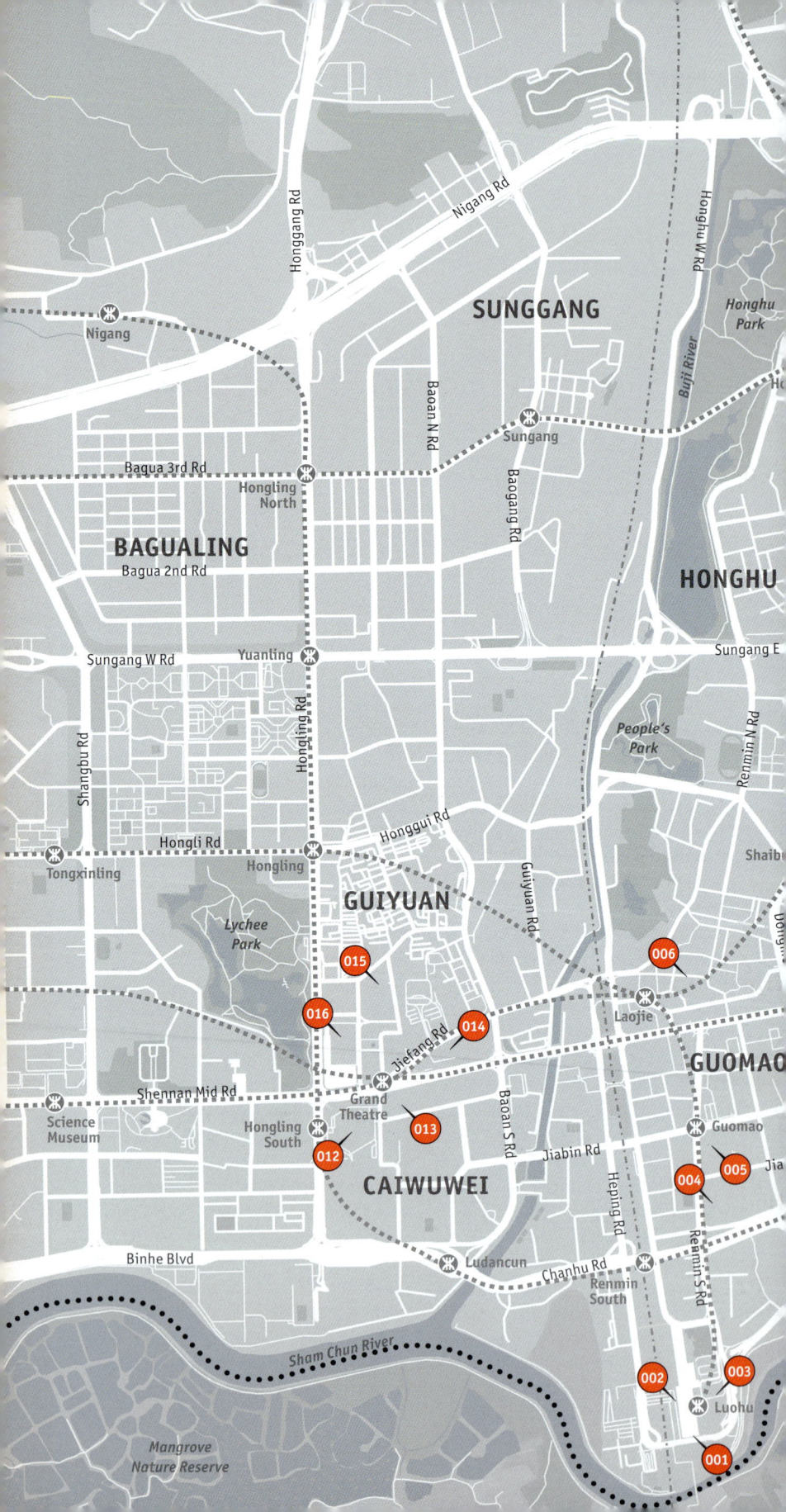

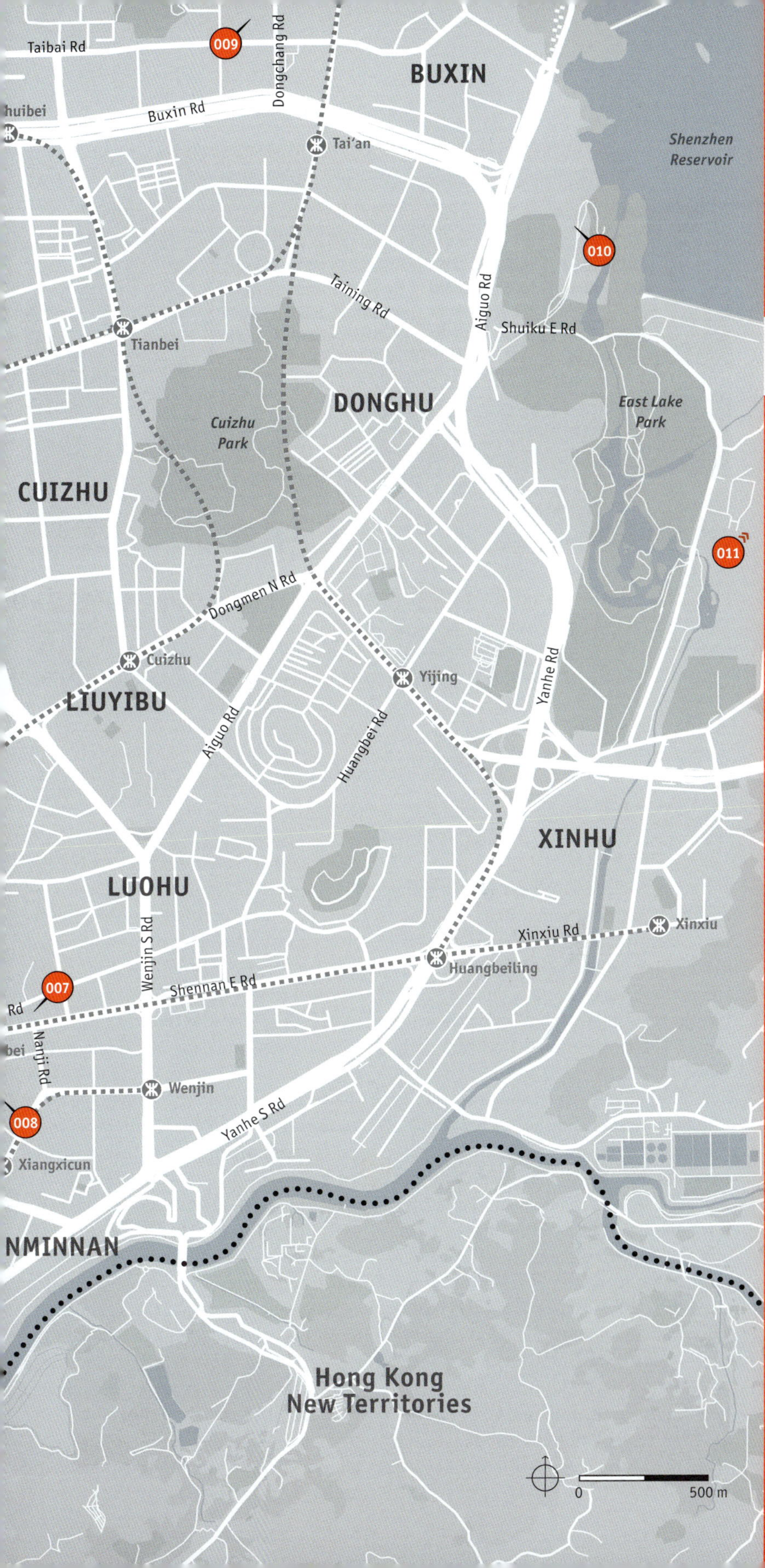

BUXIN

009

Taibai Rd

Dongchang Rd

huibei

Buxin Rd

Tai'an

Shenzhen
Reservoir

010

Aiguo Rd

Shuiku E Rd

Taining Rd

Tianbei

East Lake
Park

DONGHU

Cuizhu
Park

CUIZHU

011

Dongmen N Rd

Cuizhu

Yijing

Yanhe Rd

LIUYIBU

Aiguo Rd

Huangbei Rd

XINHU

LUOHU

Xinxiu Rd

Xinxiu

Wenjin S Rd

Huangbeiling

007

Shennan E Rd

Rd

Nanji Rd

Wenjin

bei

Yanhe S Rd

008

Xiangxicun

NMINNAN

Hong Kong
New Territories

0   500 m

Pxhere

Luohu Port Control Point ⌃   001 A

Shenzhen Port, Luohu
Unknown
1985

罗湖口岸联检大楼
罗湖区深圳罗湖口岸

 Line 1
Luohu
羅湖站

The condition for Shenzhen to be a frontier town naturally required the construction of a checkpoint physically connecting Mainland China to Hong Kong. One of the earliest governmental building realised in town was Luohu Port, which replaced the tiny pavilion from the early twentieth century built by the British. The new building reflects its unique status of 'the first gate in the south' through the reinterpretation of a traditional stylistic apparatus, which was used to design at least the external façades. The red pillars, double eaves, yellow-glazed tiles, and the archaised partition all speak an antique language that was, at that time, quite unusual and charming. Inside, continuous implementations done over the years transformed the space as needed. Nevertheless, the passage from the two territories is well marked by the pedestrian path linking the building to the Hong Kongese side of the border beyond the Shenzhen River.

Shenzhen Railway Station ⬏   002 A

1003 Jianshe Rd., Luohu
Chen Shi Min (Hua Yi Design) +
Shenzhen Machinery Institute of
Architectural Design
1989–1992

罗湖火车
罗湖区建设路1003号

Right next to Luohu Port, Chen Shi Min designed this modern Shenzhen railway station by bringing together a complex variety of technical, symbolic, and architectural instances resulting in a city landmark. The façade's glass and white tiles recall the country's southern gate, standing out from the cloudy sky as evoked by the curved concrete panels on the external curtain walls along the main façades. Laying on top of the tracks coming from Hong Kong, the station is conceived as a multi-layered building. It's accessible from the two long sides, however, the eastern side provides primary access and connectivity. An up-and-down pedestrian circulation allows for separation from vehicular and public traffic while the main concourse is located on the first floor above the tracks. Offices, restaurants, a 300-room hotel, and customs facilities complete the railway station's program, introducing a new typological mix to the Chinese panorama of railway architecture.

Luohu Shopping Mall ⪥

25 Plaza Rd., Luohu
Huasen Architectural & Engineering Designing Consultants
1989–1992

003 **A**

罗湖商业
罗湖区广场路25号

On the other side of the square and right in front of the Shenzhen Railway Station, the railway building is paired with another horizontal block that is the Luohu Shopping Mall. Since the design could not exceed the 34-metre height limit set by the station, it expands on the large site as a container ship anchored along a dock. The façade is glazed with a blue-and-white striped curtain wall. The cantilevered short sides and two barrel-vault galleries on the top recall naval shapes, while the other details reinterpret Chinese elements of traditional architecture. For example, the symmetrical main façade features a back-drawn entrance that is sustained by the system of *dougong* ('cap and block') brackets and pillars. Inside, the shopping stands selling cheap, counterfeit goods overlay the blinking interiors of this fascinating commercial maze where one can get lost in a rather disorienting experience.

International Foreign Trade Centre (Guomao Building) »

004 A

3002 Renmin S Rd., Luohu
CSADI + Chen Shi Min
(Hua Yi Design)
1985–1996

国贸大厦
罗湖区人民南路3002号

Line 1
Guomao
国贸站
20 m

Walking north on Renmin South Road from the Luohu Checkpoint, several high-rise buildings frame the street. The Guomao Building is a landmark to this day, giving the name to the surrounding area. The trade centre combines a four-storey podium containing the International Foreign Trade tower itself, plus the Tianan International Building, the Trade Commerce Building, and a high-rise apartment building. The large podium has a ground-level built on stilts so as to leave space for road circulation and access to the underground parking. The upper levels were conceived as a commercial hall with shops, restaurants, and bars lit by a glass roof. The podium opens in front of a broad pedestrian path on Renmin Road that filters the connection to the International Foreign Trade tower, a 35-storey-high building featuring offices, a luxury hotel, and a rotating restaurant on top – a national attraction at the time of its construction. The building, indeed, is a symbol. Everyone throughout the country knows the Guomao Building for being built at a speed of one storey every three days. The complex was conceived as a multi-functional venue on the wave of Western standards being imported to the newly-opened China. It is the first high-rise block of this kind, designed by a Chinese design institute that applied innovative building technologies like a large-scale slipform construction method and the first Chinese case of an aluminium-alloy glass curtain wall. The restaurant was famous for being the highest in China and one of the top 10 in the world. Dining there during his Southern Tour, Deng Xiaoping praised the 'Shenzhen Speed'.

Tianan International Building

005 A

3012 Renmin S Rd., Luohu
Chen Shi Min (Hua Yi Design) +
CEEDI
1988–1993

天安国际大厦
罗湖区人民南路3012号口

Line 1
Guomao
国贸站
180 m

Next to the Guomao Building, Chen Shi Min designed another impressive building for the sought-after Renmin Road. Following the tendency at the time, the program includes a mix of offices, apartments, a multi-functional hall, a hotel, and department stores. The commercial activities are located in the massive podium together with the independent lobbies of the other functions; in the middle of the site, a traffic corridor cuts the

ground floor from north to south, allowing secondary entrances. The podium opens onto the street with a curved multi-storey glass-glazed entrance. It sustains a U-shaped tower composed by rectangular blocks overlapped with circular terraced wings. The golden glass glaze and solid pink panels produce a unique, eye-catching result. Furthermore, as it is located on a corner block, the architect put the tower in the furthest corner of the site, creating a welcoming volume that embraces the urban space and attracts passers-by inside.

Dongmen Street

Dongmen St., Luohu
Hua Yi Design
1990s

006 **A**

东门风貌街
罗湖区东门中路

🚇 Line 1,2
Laojie
🚶 老街站
300 m

Dongmen Market Street is known in Shenzhen as the cheap shopping paradise because of the infinite number of shops and malls condensed both above and under the ground. Nevertheless, Dongmen represents the heart of the Special Economic Zone and the historical Lingnan legacy. The area was the original urban core of the early Luohu, where narrow lanes and streets were flanked by arcades featuring typical Cantonese characteristics. They are recognisable, nestled next to six large-scale buildings, mixing modern architectural elements with traditional details, such as curved pagoda roofs. One of these new developments is the Guanghua Building, which, since 1990, has housed China's first McDonald's – very telling about the pioneering history of this city during the early Open Door Policy era. In 1999, the 'Luohu Old Town Planning' initiated a deep transformation of the area, introducing car-free zones and other implementations to make Dongmen more livable.

Golden Business Centre

2028 Shennan E Rd., Luohu
Chen Shi Min (Hua Yi Design)
1994–1999

007 A

罗湖商务中心
罗湖区深南东路2028号

Line 2
Hubei

湖贝站
250 m

Looking over from the top of a high-rise building or walking on the streets of Luohu, it is hard not to stare at the eye-catching Golden Business Centre. If it were not for its showy exterior, this building would probably pass as anonymous among plenty of other classical 'architectural recipes' products. Yet, Chen Shi Min chose to clad the building in gold colour on purpose. It was meant to symbolise the business, opulence, and prosperity that was traditionally represented by golden figures and decorations. This unique appearance makes the building a landmark that changes over time as the light turns and, as it becomes more intense, produces a distorted tonal variation on the surrounding urban space as well.

(Baidu)

Luohu Art Museum

Chunfeng Rd. & Nanji Rd., Luohu
URBANUS
2007

008 A

罗湖美术馆
罗湖区春风路和南极路

Line 2
Hubei
湖贝站
400 m

Not far from the Golden Business Centre, the Luohu Art Museum is located on the site of a once shabby parking lot in a very densely populated area of Luohu. In 2000, URBANUS was asked by the Luohu Bureau of Construction Works to conceive an alternative way to design the parking lot to include a public facilities program and increase the quality of life of the local community. Through a cooperative process between administrators and architects, the site transformed according to a design that 'tries to blur the boundary of contrasting elements, such as building and plaza, indoor and outdoor, roof and ground, etc.' The parking lot was eventually converted into a sloped, semi-underground parking garage, condensed into the eastern side of the site and connected to a long gallery in the north. A glass box was built in the south-west corner and, all in the middle, the outdoor space was designed by a series of walls, sloping ponds, and floating and folding surfaces connecting the different functions at different levels. This topographic movement created a new urban geography inside the area, mimicking various climatic environments, like drylands, hilly slopes, and humid plains. This variety was also aimed to address multiple uses of the space, such as inside where galleries, art workshops, a café, and other activities coexist.

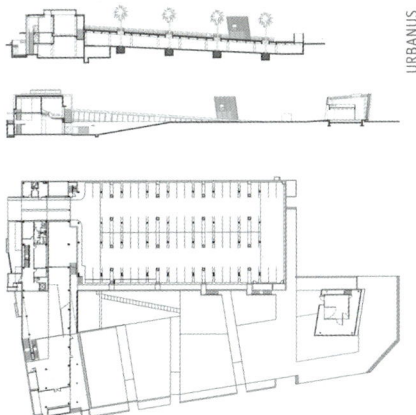

URBANUS

YUE Art Gallery ⌃
Dongchang Rd., Luohu
BLACKhome
2018

009 A

悦·艺术馆
罗湖区东昌路

 Line 5
Buxin
布心站
500 m

Shenzhen Art Museum ⌄
Donghu Park, Luohu
Shenzhen Tongji Architects
1976 (2006)

010 A

深圳美术馆
罗湖区东湖一街32号（东湖公园内）

Line 5,7
Tai'an
太安站
2 km

The YUE Art Gallery is a recent example of industrial heritage transformation. Listed in the Shenzhen Industrial Heritage Renewal Program, the original Jinwei Brewery was turned into a creative hub with exhibition halls, offices, and shops. Each building was maintained in its structure and layout while all façades were wrapped by a new skin that recalls the original curved windows. The 13-metre-high fermentation tank is the core of the site, especially at night when lights create shadows and reflections.

The founding of the Shenzhen Art Museum dates back to 1976, when it was the Shenzhen Exhibition Hall. In 1987, it was converted to an art museum focused on cultural exchange between China and foreign countries. The original building was a simple hall in a precast concrete structure covering 5,500 square metres. In 2006, the museum went through a complete makeover, and today it is a sober square box with a long glass corridor that frames the entrance square, overlooking the Shenzhen Donghu Reservoir. The combination of

H. J3755 (Wikicommons)

glass and granite contrasts with the black and white simplicity of the interiors, which is where the artworks are displayed.

Hongfa Temple ⌃

Xianhu Botanical Garden, Luohu
BLY
1985

011 A

弘法寺
罗湖区仙湖植物园内

Line 2
Xinxiu
新秀站
6.7 km

Located inside the Fairy Lake Garden on Wutong Mountain, on the eastern side of Luohu, the Hongfa Temple is the largest Buddhist temple in the Lingnan area and the first temple built in China since the founding of the People's Republic of China. Topped by orange-glazed tiled roofs, the complex of buildings composing the temple lays on the side of the mountain. The central axis organises a terraced series of halls dedicated to devotion; surrounding courtyards and other pavilions house all temple functions including a Buddhist academy, hospitality facilities, and meditation areas. Around the temple, the Fairy Lake Botanical Garden is a naturalistic reserve combining scientific research, tourism, and popular culture. Unexpectedly, there is also the Palaeontology Museum, a dinosaur-shaped venue that collects fossils found in the area.

Shenzhen Centre For Design

54

007 **Golden Business Centre**

NENT Landfill (Hong Kong)

006 **Dongmen Street**

005 **Tianan International Building**

Shennan Road

Pangling Plaza

004 Guomao Building

World Financial Centre

(Kingkey Orienta. Regent Hotel)

[photograph of buildings]

Financial Centre

012 A

5055 Shennan E Rd., Luohu
*Chen Shi Min (Watson Architecture
& Engineering Consultants)*
1986

金融中心大厦
罗湖区深南东路5055号

 Line 1,2
Grand Theatre
大剧院站
500 m

Located at the intersection of Hongling Road and Shennan Road, the Financial Centre was one of the first headquarters in the Luohu central business district, built at a time when there were open fields and manufactures all around. The building was conceived to combine two banks and a luxury hotel. To fulfil this program, Chen Shi Min designed three rectangular blocks placed at an angle of 120 degrees around a shared central space and with a common basement functioning as a pedestrian platform. This composition symbolises the spirit of unity shared by the three companies and creates a monumental object without a backside. The longitudinal façades feature a three-dimensional pattern determined by bay windows and contrasting with the curtain walls of the short sides. The multi-directional layout allows each block to have an entrance. On top of the podium, the green terrace is linked by an overpass to the nearby pedestrian network, providing a safe separation from the road traffic.

Shenzhen Development Bank »

013 A

5047 Shennan E Rd., Luohu
*Chen Shi Min (Watson Architecture
& Engineering Consultants) +
Peddle Thorp Architects*
1996

深圳发展银行大厦
罗湖区深南东路5047号

Just a few steps from the Financial Centre and Luzhi Park, in the early 1990s the so-called 'Luohu Golden Triangle' was taking shape and among the fascinating new high-rise buildings the Shenzhen Development Bank was the most iconic. The intention was to compete with the surrounding buildings and for the client to contribute to designing a building with a modern and unique outlook. At that time, Chen Shi Min was mastering a showy architectural attitude that was brought to the highest level in this work. The building rests on a modestly sized site organised according to a girdle columns grid. Above the rectangular podium, the building ascends as a pyramid-like terraced composition of blocks. The whole façade has a simple striped pattern formed by granite tiles, aluminium panels, and pink glass belt-windows. To increase the high-tech aesthetic, the building is nestled inside an upward-tilting steel structure ending in two spires. The diagonal side of the building seems to dialogue with the open space in front, creating a dramatic scenographic setting. Inside, the office space features several multi-level gardens and open-plan floors. The five-storey-high banking chamber hall is well known for being the most spacious and pleasant among all banks in Shenzhen thanks to its luxury interiors.

58

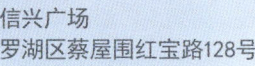

Diwang Tower
128 Hongbao Rd., Caiwuwei, Luohu
K. Y. Cheung Design Associates
1982–1985

信兴广场
罗湖区蔡屋围红宝路128号

Officially named the Shun Hing Plaza, the Diwang Tower is a symbol of the fast development of the Special Economic Zone and its economic growing power. Awarded the tallest building in Asia and the 10th tallest in the world, the building stands on the northern side of Shennan Road, at the boundary of Caiwuwei Village. It has a long-limbed profile marked by the two antennas topping the cylindric towers siding the building. The tower is paired to a triangular lower block, following the angular shape of the site and characterised by a central hole and straight belt-windows. It contrasts the blue glass glaze of the skyscraper. Inside the complex, a mixed-use program includes residential units, office space, executive clubs, and commercial halls. The 69th-floor observatory includes a museum that commemorates Shenzhen's history and provides amazing views. Due to the sandy soil of the area, the structural project features high-tech solutions for that time; indeed, it was the first steel-framed building in China since the reform era.

KK100 Kingkey Tower »
5016 Shennan E Rd., Luohu
Farrells + Arup
2012

015 A

京基100
罗湖区深南东路5016号

Located on the former site of the Caiwuwei 'village in the city', as the name anticipates, the KK100 is 100 storeys high – the fourth tallest building in the world until 2016. Such height allowed the builders to maximise the financial viability of the building, offsetting the relocation costs of the Caiwuwei villagers. It contains offices, a six-star hotel, business facilities, a sports centre, and a shopping mall. The hyperbolic glazed sky garden tops the skyscraper, creating that recognisable shape.

Shenzhen Grand Theatre ⮟
5018 Shennan E Rd., Luohu
Zong Hao Architects + AUBE + Shenzhen Institute of Beijing Construction & Planning
1989 (2004)

016 A

深圳大剧院
罗湖区深南东路5018号

The Grand Theatre is one of 'eight major cultural facilities' built in the 1980s. Located on a large square next to Diwang Tower, Shenzhen Development Bank, and the Financial Centre, it is the only horizontal building in the area. Designed as a glass box, the building was restored in 2004. The renovation replaced the original golden glass glaze with translucent bluish glass; moreover, the sunken plaza on the south-west side was eliminated, reducing the commercial functions at the ground level and enlarging the foyer. Although passers-by tend to look up at the skyscrapers around it, the theatre is a unique legacy of the low-density architecture of Shenzhen's early cultural district. It counterbalances the presence of Lychee Park on its eastern side, famous for the Deng Xiaoping billboard dedicated to his epic visit to Shenzhen and located directly in front of the theatre.

Shenzhen Centre For Design

Hong Kong New Territories

Sham Chun River

012 Financial Centre

013 Shenzhen Development Bank

Shenye Centre

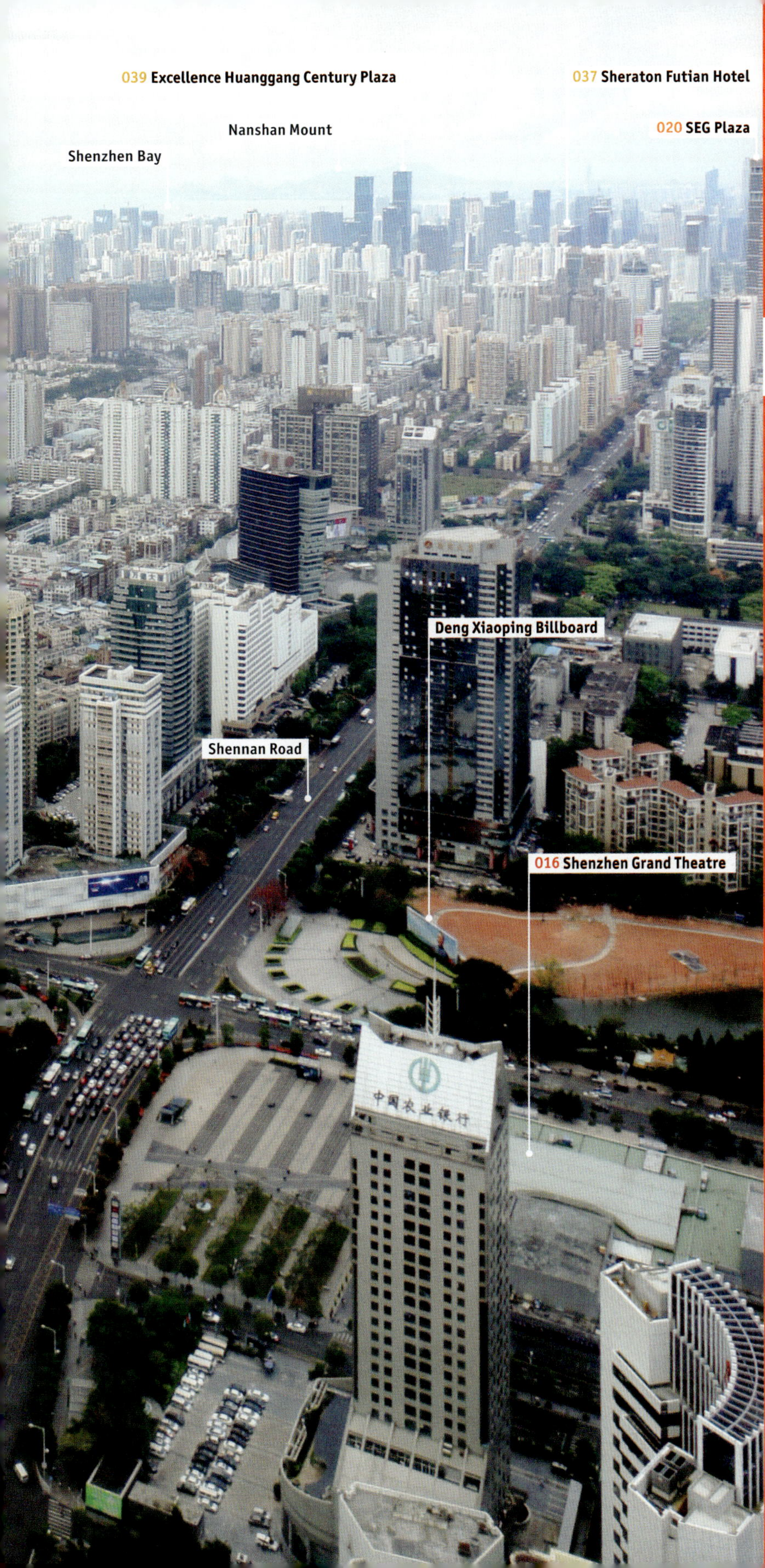
039 Excellence Huanggang Century Plaza
037 Sheraton Futian Hotel
Nanshan Mount
020 SEG Plaza
Shenzhen Bay
Deng Xiaoping Billboard
Shennan Road
016 Shenzhen Grand Theatre
中国农业银行

Frontline Underground Shopping Mall

Chip Business and Cheap Business

The urban expansion of Luohu District covered almost every free square metre in a tireless development of the rapidly saturated the area where the early Shenzhen core found its place. According to the linear urban structure, the central district of Futian was already under development in the mid-1990s, as was also the case in western Nanshan. The area between Luohu and Futian central district, specifically between Hongling Road to the east and Huanggang Road to the west, was drafted by the plan in 1978 as a mixed-use area. Three of the 'eight major cultural facilities' – Shenzhen Museum, Shenzhen Science Museum (see p. 68), and Shenzhen Hall (see p. 69) – were to each be realised nearby Lychee Park and the Grand Theatre (see p. 59), while a triangular site in the northern sector was destined for the other major facility, the Shenzhen Stadium (see p. 74). Despite the convergence of these strategic venues halfway between the two cores, from the late 1980s to the end of the century, this area became the fundamental location where most of the 'Shenzhen trading phenomenon' took place. In fact, the rest of the area has been dotted for several years by ordinary, high-density residential buildings, urban villages, manufactures, and wholesale warehouses mostly selling textile and electronic goods produced next door.

As soon as the core of the SEZ became more financially and trade-oriented, the factories moved in other northern districts of the city and out of the Special Economic Zone. This made space for the real estate market to upgrade the central areas and increase their density and value. In the 1990s, the factories moved and wholesalers rapidly expanded within the one-square-kilometre area of Huaqiangbei, the so-called 'Silicon Valley of Hardware'. Rapidly, the urban fabric changed all around the area; high-rise trading centres popped up, like the SEG Plaza (see p. 70), while covered wholesale markets occupied the basements and podium of modern tower blocks, sometimes in an infinite maze of stands selling the most incredible variety of electronic components and gadgets. Huaqiangbei is considered the first shopping street of China with 500,000 daily visitors; every electronic trader in the world knows it and has likely been there at least once.

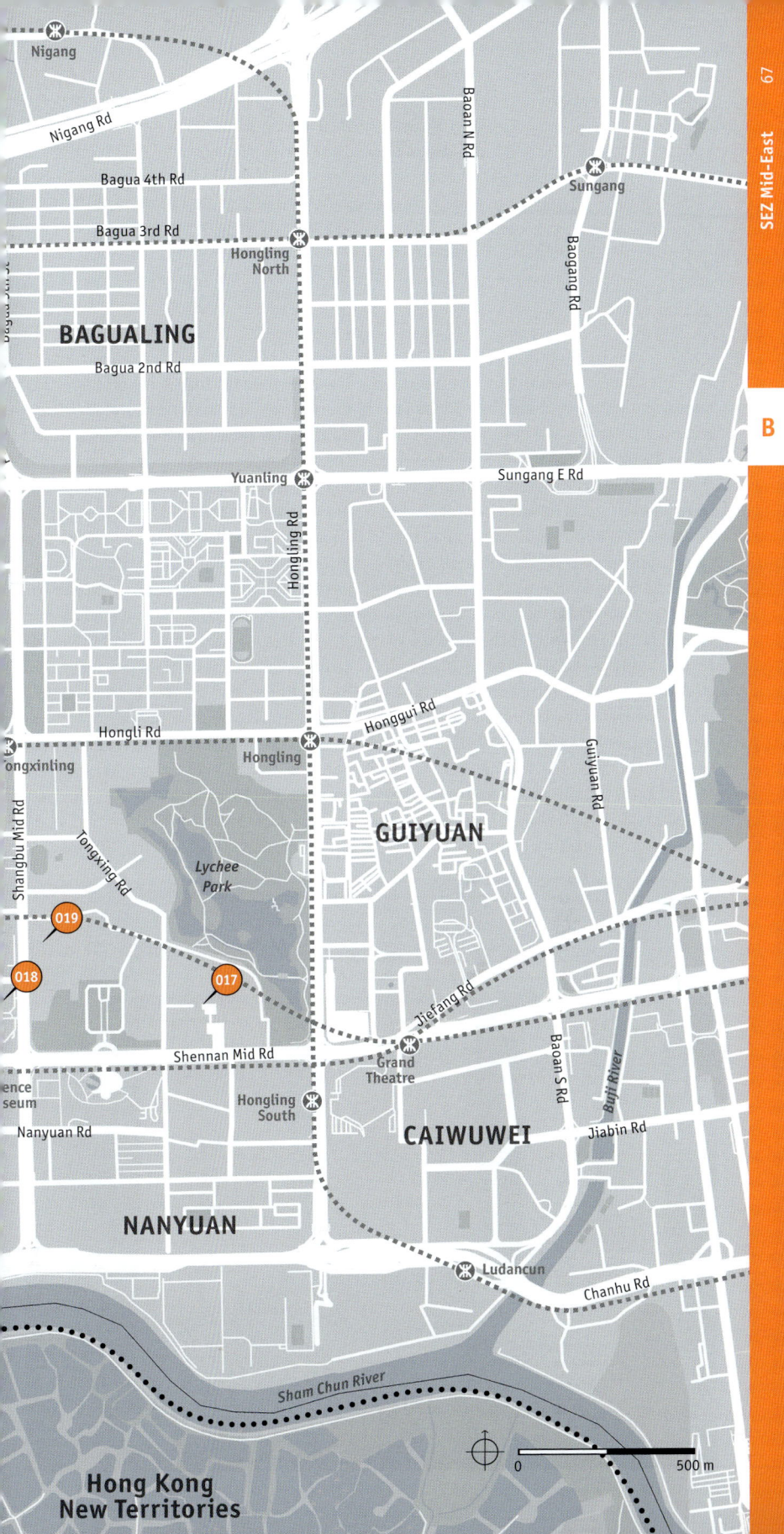

Nigang

Nigang Rd

Bagua 4th Rd

Bagua 3rd Rd

Hongling North

BAGUALING

Bagua 2nd Rd

Baoan N Rd

Sungang

Baogang Rd

Yuanling

Sungang E Rd

Hongling Rd

Hongli Rd

ongxinling

Shangbu Mid Rd

Tongxing Rd

Lychee Park

Honggui Rd

Hongling

GUIYUAN

Guiyuan Rd

019

018

017

Jiefang Rd

Shennan Mid Rd

Grand Theatre

Baoan S Rd

Buji River

ence seum

Nanyuan Rd

Hongling South

CAIWUWEI

Jiabin Rd

NANYUAN

Ludancun

Chanhu Rd

Sham Chun River

Hong Kong
New Territories

0   500 m

Shenzhen Museum ⌄ 017 B
6 Tongxin Rd., Futian
GDADRI
1981

深圳博物館
福田区同心路6号

⌘ Line 1,2
Grand Theatre
🚶 大剧院站
800 m

The Shenzhen Museum was the second public building realised in Shenzhen among the 'eight major cultural facilities' of the 1980s, following the Shenzhen Art Museum. It was designed according to a sober and straightforward composition. Outside, the solid walls sustain a concrete upper eave. At the base, a rough stone cladding creates a sort of basement running around the building. The main façade is cut vertically into three parts, where angle windows create a strong chiaroscuro and allow natural light to filter in. The main block is linked to secondary ones using these carving-like volumetric intrusions. Inside, the four-storey exhibition is organised along a spiralling inner corridor that echoes the Guggenheim Museum in New York City.

Shenzhen Science Museum » 018 B
1003 Shanqbu Middle Rd., Futian
He Jingtang (SCUT)
1987

深圳科学館
福田区上步中路1003号

⌘ Line 1
Science Museum
🚶 科学馆站
350 m

The Shenzhen Science Museum is another one of the 'eight major cultural facilities' built in the 1980s and one of the earliest science museums in China, a testament to the technological vocation of the city. One of the first buildings designed by He Jingtang, the museum is composed of a three-storey building with an octagonal larger side. On top, an octagonal ascending block houses the conference hall and stands like a traditional pagoda. The façades are all diagonal; white panels clad the building and create a clear geometry that alternate with belt windows. Inside, the museum has changed over the decades, but the layout and atmosphere are still in place, especially in the permanent exhibition which occupies 3,000 square metres.

Shenzhen Centre For Design

Shenzhen Centre For Design

Shenzhen Centre For Design

Shenzhen Hall ⌄   019 B

1006 Shangbu Middle Rd., Futian
GDADRI
1987

深圳会堂
福田区上步中路1006号

Line 1
Science Museum
科学馆站
500 m

Shenzhen Hall is one of the 'eight major cultural facilities' that architecturally embody the public dimension of the city and state. The sculptural shape of the building recalls a lithic structure composed of two blocks. The prominent one welcomes visitors with a cantilevered, covered entrance and connects with the side blocks that house offices and two auditoriums. The tectonic nature of the architectures pairs with the materials used and the art pieces decorating the gardens and interiors. Mosaic pavings, bronze and aluminium windows, oak plywood, and granite ornate this public building that is mostly unknown by citizens because of its modest size. However, it is here that the first public auction of land was held in China in 1987, marking the beginning of the 'Shenzhen Dream' and the urban development of the Special Economic Zone.

SEG Plaza

1002 N Huaqiang Rd.
Chen Shi Min (Hua Yi Design)
1995–1999

020 B

赛格广场
田区华强北路1002号

Line 1
Huaqiang Rd.
华强路站
280 m

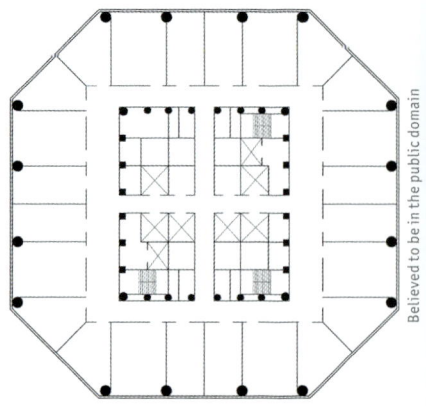

Believed to be in the public domain

SEG Plaza represents the heart of Huaqiangbei commercial area, besides being an early landmark of the Special Economic Zone. At 275 metres high, the skyscraper is octagonal in plan and stands on a square podium on a corner plot at the southern entrance of the commercial and wholesale district that specialises in electronics; it was formerly occupied by factories. At the time of construction, SEG Plaza was the tallest building in the world, conceived as a tube of reinforced concrete. All vertical connections and technical facilities are concentrated in the central core while the rest of the floor has an open plan with a ring of concrete pillars behind the curtain wall. The exterior with the grey glass cladding alternates with aluminium bands, and the antenna on top expresses the high-tech soul of the building and the business done inside. The program, indeed, is various and vertically distributed; clubs occupy the top floors, while offices stay on the upper floors, above the large podium. There, shops and wholesale stands are massed together in a three-storey semi-open market, trading 'zero-kilometre' electronic parts and products in a daily bargain. A walk around this maze of chips is unmissable.

International Science and Technology Building

Shennan Middle Rd., Futian
Chen Shi Min (Hua Yi Design)
1991–1997

021 B

国际科技大厦
福田区深南中路

 Line 1
Huaqiang Rd.
华强路站
250 m

Right in front of the SEG Plaza on the southern side of Shennan Road, another tall building designed by Chen Shi Min stands, demanding attention and distinguishing itself from the others around it. The design concept refers to the ancient belief that the universe consists of the squared earth and round sky – four dimensions and eight dimensions. The tower is composed of two intersected parallelepipeds, rotated 45 degrees, with a cubic podium and a circular rotating restaurant on top. The whole building is sustained by eight columns, eight metres apart from each other. This interpretation of tradition suggests a deepness of meanings that metaphorically endorses the commercial spirit of the building. Besides, the striped cladding is a sophisticated choice that expresses opulence and a sort of classical modernity.

View of Huaqiangbei Road

B

Shenzhen Stadium

2006 Sungang W Rd., Futian
Huasen Architectural & Engineering Designing Consultants + COX
1985

深圳体育中心
福田区笋岗西路2006号

Line 3
Tongxinling
通新岭站
1.3 km

Located in a triangular plot of land in the northern part of Yuanling District, Shenzhen Stadium was the first sports venue built in the city and one of the early strategic public facilities master planned in 1978. The centre contains several buildings and open-air sports fields. The most significant ones are the football arena, the gymnasium, and the swimming pool hall. The first is an elliptical that reinforces the concrete structure, with a two-storey outer corridor and exposed cantilevered stands, housing nearly 35,000 spectators. The second is a low, squared building with four pillars supporting a vast roof, recalling the traditional pavilion architecture. Finally, the third is the most modern building of the complex, as remarked by the steel and glass façades and the steel truss masts protruding from the roof.

China Telecom »

023 B

2001 Huafu Rd., Futian
Unknown
2004

中国电信 （深圳福田区分公司）
福田区华富路2001号

 **Line 3,7**
Huaxi
华新站
850 m

Philipp Meuser

B

In a corner plot next to the Shenzhen Central Park lake, the China Telecom building in Futian is quite recognisable for its architectural design. It's a post-modernist building, one of those designed according to the 'architectural recipes' of a Western flavour. The rectangular office block has palace-like decoration that contrasts with the agave glass glaze of the frontal tower. Instead of a bell or clock, the tower holds up antennas and satellite dishes.

Hui Hotel ↵

024 B

3015 Hongli Rd., Huaqiangbei, Futian
URBANUS / YangBangsheng & Associates Group (interior design)
2010–2014

回酒店
福田区华强北红荔路3015号

 **Line 3,7**
Huaxi
华新站
450 m

Near Huaqiangbei Street, the Hui Hotel is an example of post-industrial regeneration of a former electronic factory. The

fashion commissioning company wanted the architects to follow the fashion theme. Thus, by wrapping the existing building with a three-dimensional skin, the façades seem clad with a bright fabric. Inside, the wooden boiserie and furniture reproduce the same effect in a warm, soft version.

Alex Chan

Alex Chan

The Shenzhen River, the natural boundary between Hong Kong (left) and Shenzhen (right)

SEZ Mid
Futian Central District

Shenzhen Civic Centre (see p. 90)

The Ultimate Champs-Élysées

Both the municipal and the state governments held the great expectation that Shenzhen would compete with any first-class city in the world. They wanted it and were ready to make any resource available to achieve this goal. It was of national importance to show that China could look forward to the future and embrace the global bets towards economic growth, sustainability, technological development, trading ascendancy, and cultural production. The various fields in which Shenzhen was willing to excel have kept both the public and private actors busy and, at the same time, conscious that the fame of this newborn city should be built step by step, starting from its physical palimpsest.

Already in 1978, the first urban plan of the Special Economic Zone outlined the future location of a central district, Futian, in the middle of Luohu, the early centre of trade and government institutions, and Nanshan, with its port and university. At that time, the plan simply indicated this project without detailing the consistency nor the specific program that Futian Central District should eventually have. It was the master plan of 1984 that put forward a proposal for the Futian Central District in the core area kept free from the rapid expansion of real estate.

Geographically speaking, the site was unique; a plain land of nearly 200 square hectares surrounded by Lianhua Mountain in the north and Shenzhen Bay in the south, and enclosed by four major roadways: Binhe Avenue, Lianhua Road, Caitian Road, and Xinzhou Road. It is the natural barycentre of the SEZ and the most strategic location in terms of connections within the city, such as with Hong Kong and the territories northward. According to the plan, the Futian Central District was destined to become Shenzhen's main business and cultural area, as well as the 'postcard' image of a memorable contemporary city.

Despite the local attitude in favour of fast-building, it took a decade to bring the project to maturity. The government pressure was very high and their expectations had become as high as imaginable. In 1996, a new master plan drafted a new programmatic document announcing the 'Overview Urban Design and Architectural Design in Shenzhen Central District'. According to the plan, Futian Central District was conceived as 'a modern international city, a regional economic centre

Lee/Timchula Architects (china-up.com)

Futian Central District master plan, 1996

city, and a garden city'. These three con-notations condense the challenging in-tention to showcase the Chinese New-Era competitiveness all in one. The trading nature of the city would obviously find the location for locate private headquar-ters, financial hubs, and commercial fa-cilities here. The natural characteristics of the site would be an advantage to the creation of a green network with ecolog-ical features. Moreover, the yet-to-be-built cultural institutions that Shenzhen needed would eventually find their best place in the centre of the city.

At the end of 1995, the Shenzhen Urban Planning Commission announced an in-ternational design competition for Futian Central District. Eminent foreign design-ers were invited to participate with their proposals and, in the organisers' per-spective, this was a great opportunity for ensuring high standards of urban design in addition to being acknowledged by the global media.

The quality and recognition that this pro-ject was to bring to Shenzhen was of pri-mary importance to governors and lo-cal stakeholders. Both international and well-known local planners and de-sign experts were invited to participate as jury members as well. Among the pro-posals, the jury awarded Lee/Timchula

Architects' plan, followed by Chen Shi Min's one which had several intuitions in common with the winner.

Lee/Timchula Architects' project draft-ed a comprehensive solution to harmo-nise the general layout, structural grid, traffic networks, architectural image, and it foresaw some grade of future imple-mentation and improvement. It stress-es the north-south axis connecting Lianhuashan at the north and Shenzhen River at the south and defines a symmetri-cal layout based on the original road grid. This grid divides the site into a north-ern hilly park, a 250-metre-wide central green belt, condensing the large-scale venues, and a series of smaller blocks on the eastern and western sides designat-ed mainly to commerce and offices, with a minor quota of high-rise residential developments. The northern section of the central green belt identifies the fu-ture Central Cultural District where later the Shenzhen Civic Centre (see p. 90), also designed by Lee/Timchula Archi-tects with its curved roof perpendic-ular to the north-south axis, the Chil-dren's Palace (see p. 94), the Shenzhen Library and Concert Hall (see p. 92), and the Museum of Contemporary Art & Planning Exhibition (see p. 93) would all find a place. The southern section and the blocks along its boundary are des-tined to the Central Business District where a series of impressive skyscrap-ers will later compose the new skyline of Futian; here, the horizontal volume of the Shenzhen Convention and Exhibi-tion Centre (see p. 104) marks the end point of the north-south axis, thus acting as the counterpart to Lianhuashan Park (see p. 94) to the north.

The second place awarded Chen Shi Min, instead, suggested a comparison be-tween this site, the layout of Wangcheng ideal city, and the Beijing complex of the Forbidden City and Tiananmen Square, creating a superimposed grid and similar proportions between built volumes and urban voids. The search for a well-known reference was essential, after all, to put the project at a high level of engagement with competitors, to self-create that 'au-ra' of success Shenzheners were seek-ing, and to bridge a significant cultural

C

辛桂鵬

View of the Futian Central District from Lianhuashan peak

domain, no matter the time or space. Connecting to the Chinese conception of urban space was certainly fundamental for declaring Shenzhen the contemporary descendant of the country's millenary heritage; meanwhile, the desire to stand out globally naturally explained the logic behind the search for foreign endorsements. However, the Central District had to be monumental – a new, secular Campidoglio that could remain a stamp on everyone's mind, like the Pudong in Shanghai

Zhang Chao – Courtesy URBANUS

Top view of the Central Cultural District

Futian skyline from Futian Civic Centre

or the National Mall in Washington, where citizens could find the local cultural roots manifested. With these ambitions, the central green belt became a linear park conceived as a multi-layered structure accommodating cultural and mobility facilities below the terraced level of the park. This green corridor leading to Lianhuashan Mountain is, indeed, a continuous promenade that gives access to a variety of indoor and outdoor episodes.

In 1997, Japanese architect Kisho Kurokawa was commissioned for the detailed master plan of the central green axis and of the overall landscape design of the site. In his plan, Kurokawa aimed to combine the urban and human scales according to different spatial and functional layers for a result comparable to internationally renowned urban centres, like the promenade from the Louvre to the Champs-Élysées in Paris. Kurokawa himself designed the BookCity mall (see p. 94) according to this symbiotic concept contributing to the construction of a three-dimensional outdoor space. The plan was confirmed, improved, and implemented over the years, up to the recent completion of the Shenzhen Civic Centre Shi Yuan & Li Yuan (see p. 91) by URBANUS, as known as the green square found in the middle of the Central Cultural

District. The horizontality of this central green corridor creates a huge disorienting space, although clearly perceivable as a unique space, that spans as far as the eye can see, all the way to the crown of high-rise buildings bordering the site.

Since the 1996, the area has been a never-ending construction site. Record-breaking buildings, like the Ping'an International Finance Centre (see p. 107), have tirelessly modified the skyline in a variety of forms, styles, and innovative solutions designed by local and international architects. At first glance, it is impressive, with the Civic Centre at the centre, reaching all the way to the far New Territories of Hong Kong to the south as well as the highest skyscrapers in Luohu and Nanshan and the mountain beyond. In a multi-scale logic, Kurokawa foresaw the creation of a metropolitan green corridor connecting Futian Central District to the mountains on the SEZ's northern border, according to the wider 'Eco-Media City Project Plan' he drafted for Shenzhen. In recent decades, this idea of interrelated green networks has become crucial in the conservation of Shenzhen's green land and preservation of its natural resources in terms of a sustainability discourse and a practical need to control pollution and soil consumption.

Zhang Chao – Courtesy URBANUS

037 **Sheraton Futian Hotel**

039 **Excellence Huanggang Century Plaza**

035 **China Guangdong Nuclear Headquarters**

Hong Kong

028 **MOCAPE**

025 **Shenzhen Civic Centre**

030 **Children's Palace**

029 **BookCity**

Futian Central District from Lianhuashan

38 Shenzhen Convention and Exhibition Centre

041 Ping'an International Finance Centre

044 Duty Free Building

046 Shenzhen Stock Exchange

045 SBF Tower

027 Shenzhen Library and Concert Hall

026 Shenzhen Civic Centre Shi Yuan & Li Yuan

Hongli Road

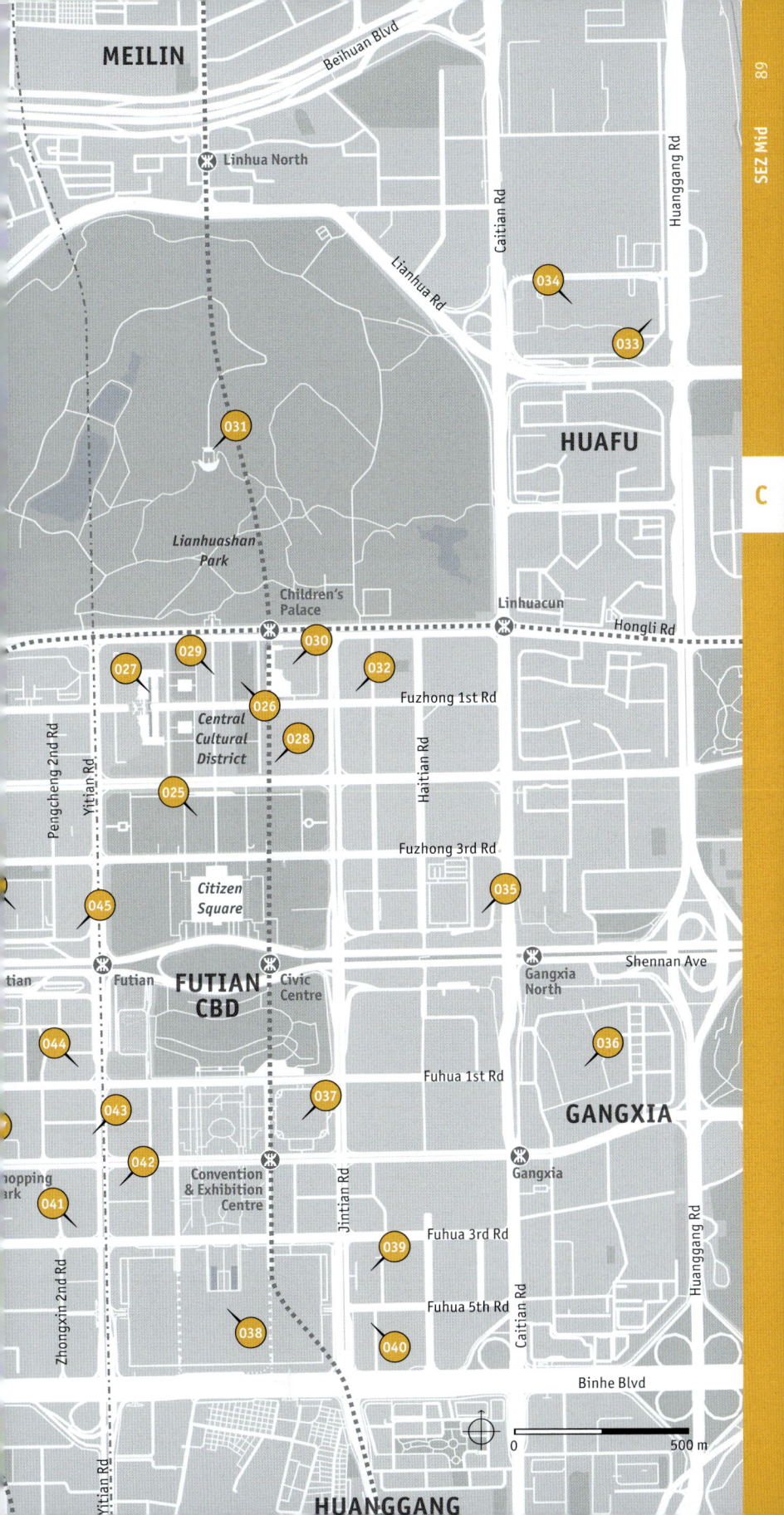

MEILIN

Beihuan Blvd

Linhua North

Caitian Rd

Lianhua Rd

Huanggang Rd

034

033

HUAFU

031

Lianhuashan
Park

Children's
Palace

Linhuacun

Hongli Rd

Pengcheng 2nd Rd

Yitian Rd

029

027

030

026

032

Fuzhong 1st Rd

Central
Cultural
District

028

Haitian Rd

025

Fuzhong 3rd Rd

Citizen
Square

045

035

Futian

Futian

FUTIAN
CBD

Civic
Centre

Gangxia
North

Shennan Ave

036

044

GANGXIA

043

037

Gangxia

042

Jintian Rd

Convention
& Exhibition
Centre

hopping
ark

041

Fuhua 1st Rd

Fuhua 3rd Rd

039

Zhongxin 2nd Rd

Caitian Rd

038

040

Fuhua 5th Rd

Binhe Blvd

0   500 m

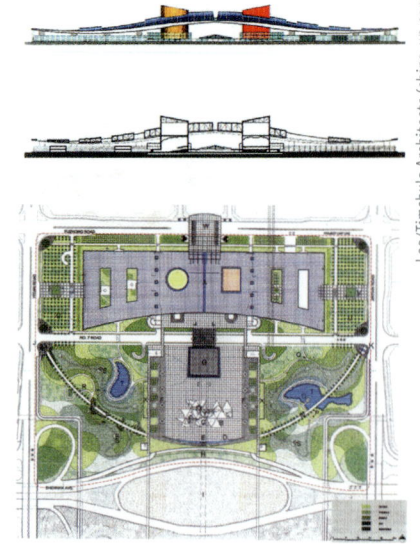

Shenzhen Civic Centre ⌃

Shennan Ave., Futian
Lee/Timchula Architects + SZAD
1999

025 C

市民广场
福田区深南大道口

Line 2,4
Civic Centre
市民中心站
100 m

In 1996, when the plan for the Shenzhen Central District was mature and ready to be fully realised, an international design competition was held to define the architectural solution for the most significant building of the area: the later-named Shenzhen Civic Centre. Among the several proposals drafted by eminent architects, American firm Lee/Timchula Architects drew a maniloquent architectural landmark capable of holding the urban scale of the whole district. The building, indeed, occupies a barycentric position on the central axis, pivoting the Central Cultural District to the north and the rest of the CBD to the south. The huge horizontally stretched volume and the unique shape of the big curved roof reinterpret the ancient typology of the pavilion in a post-modernist way, as declared by the combination of colours, materials, and geometries. The body pavilion seems inexistent, if not for the two gigantic towers intersecting the curved mesh of the roof, sustained by a truss structure system anchored by the multi-storey podium. The functional program is housed accordingly, to separate the governance offices from the city museum and exhibition halls. The void between roof and podium frames the landscape straight from Lianhuashan Park (see p. 94) at the north and the Shenzhen Convention and Exhibition Centre (see p. 104) at the south. This creates a visual continuity that recalls the figure of a city gate and gives the building a good *fengshui*.

Lee/Timchula Architects (china-up.com)

C

Shenzhen Civic Centre
Shi Yuan & Li Yuan ⥥
Hongli Rd., Futian CBD, Futian
URBANUS
2019

026 C

深圳市民中心诗园礼园
福田区福田ＣＢＤ

The open area in the middle of the Central Cultural District has been waiting for a final landscape design for three decades, despite all master plans that predetermined the program to be pursued. After the completion of all the pieces of architecture composing the venue, URBANUS was eventually commissioned to redefine the landscape design of this vast space, aiming to improve the outdoor facilities and quality of the public space. In doing so, they reshaped the walking path on the BookCity roof deck, harmonising it with the rest of the square. The eastern and western sides, separated along the central axis by the mall, feature different botanical gardens and plenty of micro-situational designs that improve the daily use by citizens of every age. Besides boosting the aesthetical value of the area, this green square has suddenly turned to be a lively place where people gather and find refreshment from the hot local climate.

Zhang Chao

Zhang Chao

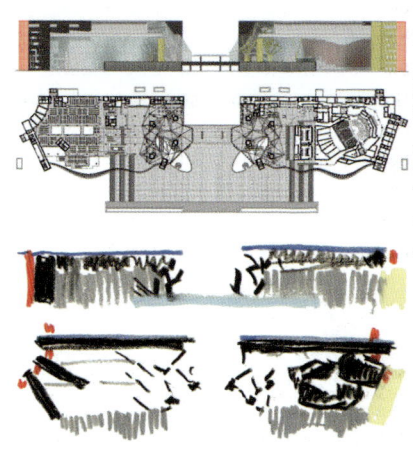

Shenzhen Library and Concert Hall

027 **C**

Fuzhong First Rd., Futian
Arata Isozaki & Associates + BIAD
1997–2007

深圳音乐厅店 – 深圳图书馆
福田区福中一路

Line 3,4
Children's Palace
少年宫站
400 m

On the western side of the green belt of the Central Cultural District, a complex of twin buildings houses two of the leading cultural institutions of the city: the Shenzhen Library and Concert Hall. Designed by Japanese Pritzker Prize winner

Arata Isozaki, the project shows an almost stereometric composition aligned along the east-west axis of Fuzhong First Road which runs below the elevated entrance square, hidden behind a black stone-clad wall waterfall. Each building has a multifaceted crystal-shaped main façade, which is framed at the external edge by a coloured tower block that continues on the backside, turning into a black solid blind wall. Inside, the naturalist metaphors continue with the structural 'forest of pillars' reinterpreting treelike shapes. The library has a multi-level reading room with snaky hanging walkways overlooking the central green belt. In the concert hall, the Symphony Hall has a vineyard configuration as a 'canyon terrace'. The essentiality of the matters and sense of openness create a variety of relaxing interiors, evoking a spiritual silence in contrast with the tumultuous energy of the city.

Museum of Contemporary Art & Planning Exhibition (MOCAPE) `028` `C`

184 Fuzhong Rd., Lianhua St., Futian
Coop Himmelb(l)au
2007–2016

深圳市当代艺术与城市规划馆
福田区莲花街道福中路184号口

On the eastern side of the Central Cultural District, the master plan allocated two independent museums: the Children's Palace and the MOCAPE. The latter was designed by the Austrian firm Coop Himmelb(l)au, winner of the related competition in 2007. The concept was to combine two separated venues, the art museum (MOCA) and the planning exhibition (PE) under the same shell with a set of jointly used facilities, including a lobby, conference rooms, and an auditorium. This separation allows for efficient organisation of their functional and technical requirements, while the fluid space folded around serves as a sort of public square where plenty of things happen at the same time. Ramps, stairs, and an escalator give access to different levels and exhibitions, offering impressive views on the 17-storey-high internal void, almost free of columns. White shiny surfaces reflect the light and the objects, creating mirroring effects of ephemeral beauty. The monolithic mesh of the building diverges from the other venues of the area, revealing the digital mastery of the architects' language. The glass portions of the façade contrast with the solid metal clad of the less-public portions of the building, generating such a sculptural object.

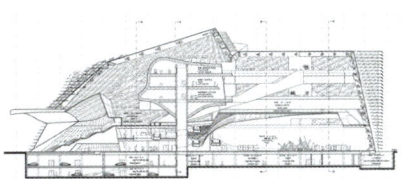

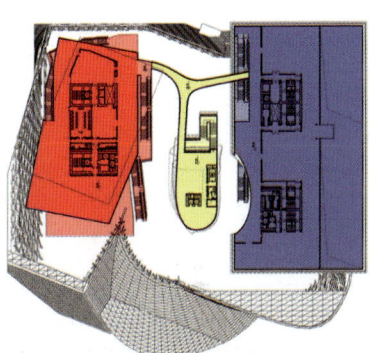

Coop Himmelb(l)au

`C`

Dietertimmerman (Flickr - CC BY 2.0)

Dietertimmerman (Flickr - CC BY 2.0)

BookCity ⌃
Fuzhong First Rd., Futian
Kisho Kurokawa
1998

`029 C`

深圳书城
福田区莲花街道福中社区福中一路

Laying along the symmetrical axis of the Central Cultural District, BookCity is a partially underground shopping mall directly accessible from the subway. Linking the Civic Centre to Lianhuashan Park from south to north, the 25-metre-wide roof acts as long pedestrian path, creating an elevated terrace that overlooks the museums and public spaces around it. The building itself seems to mostly dematerialise from sight thanks to the flourishing greenery, achieving Kisho Kurokawa's idea of 'returning to nature'.

Children's Palace ↳
Fuzhong First Rd., Futian
*Lee/Timchula Architects +
Zong Hao Architects*
2004

`030 C`

深圳少年宫
深圳市福田区福中一路市少年宫

Shenzhen's children's museum is not exactly a fairy-tale domain. Rather, it is a scientific learning centre accommodated in a post-constructivist building composed by a combination of polyhedra, cylindric, and spheric volumes. The asperity of the composition gives a high-tech aesthetic, as seen in the steel structures and glass curtain walls that characterise the entrance halls.

Lianhuashan Park
Hongli Rd., Futian CBD, Futian
Kisho Kurokawa
1997

`031 C`

莲花山公园
福田区福田CBD

 Line 3
Linhuacun
莲花村站
400 m

At the very north end of the Central Cultural District's green belt, a high hill frames the landscape and acts as a

辛桂鹏

C

magnificent background to Futian's urban scenography. Lianhuashan Park recalls the cosmological figure of a mountain; it protects the settlement from the adverse northern winds and counterbalances the water streams at the south – a metaphor of the Shenzhen River. Conceived as the head of the whole master plan of Futian, the park itself is a commemorative place of president Deng Xiaoping, whose statue stands on the peak overlooking the city. The natural biodiversity is plentiful and the panoramic view on Shenzhen is well worth the climb.

stressing the third dimension, with a climax achieved by a deep vertical cut dividing a thin slice of the glass box from the rest of the mass. On top, the last floors house a cylindrical clubhouse that offers a dramatic view of the CBD. The simplicity of the forms and matters also designs the minimalistic interiors dominated by the geometrical composition of both public and private spaces.

Shenzhen Metro Headquarters Tower

032 C

1016 Fuzhong First Rd., Futian
URBANUS
2005

深圳地铁大厦
福田区福中一路1016号

Line 3,4
Children's Palace
少年宫站
260 m

Yang Chaoying

Not far from the public venues of the Civic Centre, URBANUS's Shenzhen Metro Headquarters Tower stands like a glass stele on the edge of the road, almost hiding the large solid pavilion linked to it. The sobriety and solemnity of this building make it stand out, not even competing with the other high-rise towers around. The bluish glass curtain wall that covers most of the façades is patterned by straight lines

Futian from Shum Yip Upperhills

Shum Yip Upperhills

5001 Huanggang Rd., Futian
Skidmore, Owings & Merrill
2013–2017

033 C

深业上城T2写字楼
福田区皇岗路5001号

Line 3
Linhuacun
莲花村站
1.4 km

Located on the eastern side of Lianhuashan Park, this extensive site – destined to become a mixed-use development – was commissioned to a bench of architects who designed a group of towers, pavilions, commercial halls, and public spaces. On the eastern side of the site, American firm Skidmore, Owings & Merrill was commissioned to design two supertall towers and a ballroom pavilion. Their goal for all the three buildings was to provide sweeping views of the city by minimising the structural impact and creating a strong link with the timeless aesthetic of the city's surrounding skyline. The tallest tower is 80 storeys high and accommodates offices and a luxury hotel at the top. The ballroom pavilion features two party rooms and a breathtaking outdoor public terrace facing an elevated public garden and linked to the two pedestrian bridges which cross the site towards the nearby Beacon Hill Park.

Shum Yip Upperhills LOFT »

5001 Huanggang Rd., Futian
URBANUS
2018

034 C

深业上城 LOFT
福田区皇岗路5001号

As part of Shum Yip Development, architect URBANUS was asked to design a mixed-use compound on top of the 60,000 square metres of shopping mall in the area framed by the skyscrapers of SOM and others. The design aimed to counterbalance the verticality of the nearby high-rise towers and connect to the natural landscape of the hills and mountains that frame Futian at the north. With this dual goal, the architects realised a multifunctional and multi-density settlement that recalls their long research on new forms of urban development able to withstand the future growth of high-density cities like Shenzhen. Recalling this research on urban density conducted over

ZtpVision

the years, URBANUS created two artificial mountain volumes on the boundary of the site, enclosing a matrix of three-to-four-storey lofts in the shape of a small town. A suspended walking path increases the complexity of the pedestrian circulation, connecting private and semi-private areas to the shared facilities located in the mountain blocks and linking the inner core of the side to the outer urban park.

The sloping roofs filter the natural light inside the 'village'. The variety of combinations generated by subtraction of the built volumes and voids defines a human-scale micro-urban landscape framed by the artificial mountains.

URBANUS

ZtpVision

Yang Chaoying

China Guangdong Nuclear Headquarters Building

Shennan Ave. & Caitian Rd., Futian
URBANUS
2008–2015

中广核大厦
福田区深南路与彩田路交汇处西北侧

035 **C**

Line 4
Gangxia North
岗厦北站
200 m

Among the recent buildings completed in the northern section of the CBD, the CGN Headquarters seems far from the typical 'eloquence of power'. The simplicity of its façade conveys a new digital aesthetic thanks to modular squared windows that, varied across the surface, define the architectural language. The complex is composed of two distinct blocks that form a bracket in the air while a modular grid shapes the interior layout like the exterior. The concept of tension and variation is a metaphor for the nuclear energy industry inside. By night, the dark metal façade is even more expressive; light travels through it, transforming it into an infinitely changing crystalline skin.

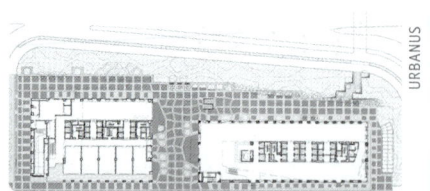

URBANUS

Alex Chan

Alex Chan

Gangxia Village

Gangxia, Futian
Informal Settlement
1980s–1990s

岗厦村
福田区岗厦村

Line 1
Gangxia
岗厦站
350 m

C

Before the construction of the real estate developments that compose Futian Central Business District, the area was almost entirely agricultural except for the presence of a few rural villages, like Gangxia, that, over time, transformed into dense 'villages within the city'. Walking across the maze of 'handshake buildings' is an extraordinary chance to see the contrasts between these settlements and the rest of the city in terms of scale, public uses, rules, and habits. Most of its inhabitants work in the CBD and rent affordable housing here. Most of the original fabric of the villages has been destroyed to make space for the planned development, resulting in the rectification and reduction of Gangxia's boundaries. The battle between villagers, stakeholders, and private companies has been firing up the debate on whether and how to preserve the village. In this confrontation, several architects have proposed experimental ways to rejuvenate and transform the village, but the issue is still open.

© Mapbox, © OpenStreetMap

041 **Ping'an International Finance Centre**

Greater China IFC

051 **China Merchants Bank Tower**

Hilton

035 China Guangdong Nuclear Headquarters

3 Shenzhen Broadcasting Centre

045 SBF Tower

046 Shenzhen Stock Exchange

C

CGN

Shennan Road

Sheraton Futian Hotel (Great China International Exchange Square) ⌃
037 C

1 Fuhua First Rd., Futian
Anbao Design + Archurban
2005

深圳大中华喜来登酒店
福田区福华一路1号

Line 1,4
Convention and Exhibition Centre
会展中心站
100 m

On the south-east corner of the CBD central park, the master plan reserved a plot of land for one of the most extravagant buildings realised in town. With a unique profile characterised by multi-angular 'feather-like arcs', the Great China International Exchange Square was designed to impress as the architectural icon of Shenzhen. On a massive square podium, three tower blocks compose a metaphorical 'south-facing throne', culminating in a reversed curved-roof crown. The black glass glazing contrasts with the white vertical profiles framing the podium and the central wing of the northern block, in a sculptural way that creates a dramatic effect once lit up at night. Inside, the central hall is an enormous record-setting columnless space, also memorable for its decorative extravaganza.

Shenzhen Convention and Exhibition Centre »
038 C

Fuhua Third Rd., Futian
gmp Architekten
2004

深圳会展中心
福田区福华三路口

Line 1,4
Convention and Exhibition Centre
会展中心站
600 m

Winner of the related design competition in 2001, gmp Architekten participated in the construction of one of the main architectural objects composing the scenographic central axis of the Futian CBD. This gigantic flat building of 280 × 540 metres lays at the southern end of the symmetrical urban layout of the district, not far from the Shenzhen River. It represents the horizontal counterpart to the hilly Lianhuashan Park aligned at the north. The visitors' level is located above ground, to separate logistical traffic, and sky bridges connect it to the nearby urban elevated pedestrian network. The nine exhibition halls are interconnected as to create differently sized halls as needed. A-shaped steel trestle structures frame the space at intervals of 30 metres and rises to almost 60 metres. A tube-shaped congressional building hovers above the exhibition platform.

Excellence Huanggang Century Plaza »
039 C

2030 Jintian Rd., Futian
Leo A. Daly + CCDI
2009

卓越世纪中心
福田区金田路2030号

Located at the eastern side of the Exhibition Centre, on a modest rectangular plot, the Excellence Huanggang Century Plaza is known as the 'Twin Towers' and is one of the 'Dancing Dragons' developments composing the southern CBD's super high-rise area. The project combines four independent towers at the corners of the plot, with a shared open square in the

Mx. Granger (Wikicommons – CC0 1.0)

middle. The two towers at the north are the tallest even among the surroundings. The agave glass curtain wall covering all façades seems to be carved as a diamond, with regular diagonal folds along each side. The peculiar treatment of the façade makes the towers iconic, especially when they are lit up at night.

Posasihumwioa (Wikicommons CC BY-SA 4.0)

BIG - Bjarke -ngels Group

Zhang Chao

Zhang Chao

Shenzhen Energy HQ «

040 C

2026 Jintian Rd., Futian
Bjarke Ingels Group
2008

深圳能源大廈
福田区金田路2026号

Designed for the state-owned Shenzhen Energy Company, BIG developed a building that naturally stands out from the urban fabric of the south-east CBD. The U-shape is composed by two towers, with one the double of the other in terms of width, and a common podium with public facilities and the lobbies. The glass and steel façades generate very bright interiors, while the stone and wood warm up the minimal design of the working spaces. The glass envelope has an undulating profile that creates an fascinating rippled skin. Besides breaking the monotony of the façade, it contributes to solar shading management and reduction of the energy consumption. At the base, the glass skin seems to open and welcome visitors inside the lobbies. On the high levels, the façade's deformations offer different views over the city and were destined for special uses, such as executive clubs and resting areas. As the glass changes its transparency at sunset, the façade's curved parts create an 'almost wood-like texture' that lights up artificially.

Ping'an International Finance Centre ↱

041 C

5033 Yitian Rd., Futian
Kohn Pedersen Fox Associates
2017

平安国际金融中心
福田区益田路5033号

Line 1,3
Shopping Park
购物公园
350 m

With a height of 599 metres, the Ping'an International Finance Centre is the fourth tallest building in the world and the second tallest in Asia. It is 115 storeys high with a total floor area of nearly 500,000 square metres, occupied by offices and business facilities. The gigantic

(Bigstock)

tower stands on the south-west side of the Futian CBD, right next to the Coco Park entertainment area and the high-speed underground railway station. The vertical profile is cut like a gemstone ending in a pyramidal observatory. Glass, chevron-shaped, and stone-clad, the façades partially reveal the internal complexity of the structural system. The large podium opens on a wide street corner from which one is hardly able to look up to the top of the building due to its height. By contrast, on clear days, it is visible from as far as the hills of both Longgang and Bao'an districts.

Bird's-eye view of Futian and Luohu

033 Shum Yip Upperhills

035 China Guangdong Nuclear Headquarters

032 Shenzhen Metro Headquarters Tower

Longgang

043 Shenzhen Broadcasting Centre

025 Shenzhen Civic Centre

Shennan Road

046 Shenzhen Stock Exchange

041 **Ping'an International Finance Centre**

038 **Shenzhen Convention and Exhibition Centre**

039 **Excellence Huanggang Century Plaza**

014 **Diwang Tower**

007 **Golden Business Centre**

015 **KK100**

Hong Kong

042 **Excellence Group Times Plaza**

C

Wu Qiwei

Excellence Group Times Plaza `042` `C`
4068 Yitian Rd., Futian
URBANUS
2010

卓越时代广场
福田区益田路4068号

Line 1,4
Convention and Exhibition Centre
会展中心站
100 m

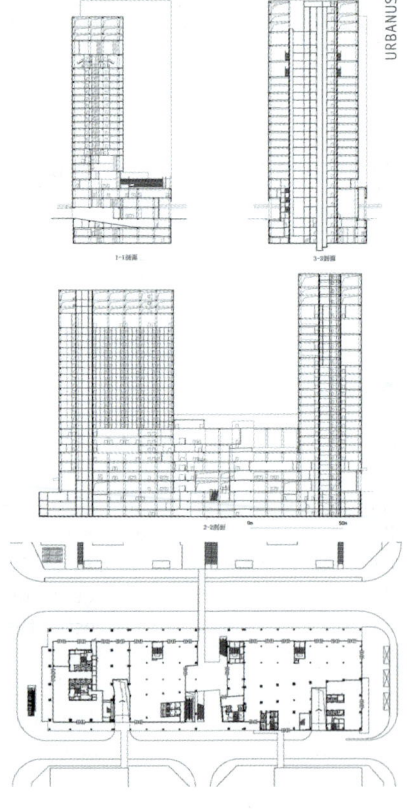

URBANUS

Designed by the local studio URBANUS, this mixed-use complex stands between the forest of skyscrapers, right in front of the west side of the Yijing Central Walk shopping mall. At first sight, the continuous profile of the two towers inflecting into the podium as a fragmented ribbon makes this building quite different from the others in the area. URBANUS's concept was to create an above-ground interconnection between the surrounding blocks and the shopping mall, providing a transitional facility thanks to the commercial podium. This increased the length of upper-street pedestrian paths in a continuous system reaching Lianhuashan Park. Looking at the main façade, the perspective suggests the three-dimensional complexity of the project. Indeed, the double L-shape of the building extends the horizontal dimension of the green-roofed mall, anticipating the verticality of the surrounding towers.

(Bigstock)

Philipp Meuser

Shenzhen Broadcasting Centre 043 C
5055 Yitian Rd., Futian
SZAD
2001

信息枢纽大厦
福田区益田路5055号

Line 1,3
Shopping Park
购物公园
200 m

Although it dates back to just 2001, the Broadcasting Centre represents the architectural prototype of the mid-1990s. With its structuralist language influenced by the works of Norman Foster, the building breaks up the monotony of ordinary office blocks, the rigour of classicist typologies, and any relation with the context. The 8-storey podium holds the main 48-storey tower as well as a 22-storey annex. The boat-shape of the building is evident. Meanwhile, the curved profile of the tower seems to be standing in the bow of the boat, sustained by the steel mast of the lifts.

Duty Free Building 044 C
6 Fuhua First Rd., Futian
Tongji Architectural Design
2001

免税大厦
福田区福华一路6

Line 2,3,11
Futian
福田站
300 m

Overlooking Futian CBD's central park, the Duty Free Building stands out among the glass-and-steel skyscrapers for its Deco aesthetic, recalling more so the Shanghaiist architecture of the 1930s than the futuristic image of its nearby counterparts. Coherent with the opulent interiors, the exterior is indeed defined by the stereometric traction of volumetric parts. This creates a strong chiaroscuro and relieves the building of its weighty appearance. Vertical windows fill the façades from the bottom to the top, where a glass crown lights up the sky hall, emphasising the verticality of the building.

SBF Tower

5999 Yitian Rd., Futian
Hans Hollein &
Christoph Monschein
2018

基金大厦
福田区益田路5999号

Line 2,3,11
Futian

福田
250 m

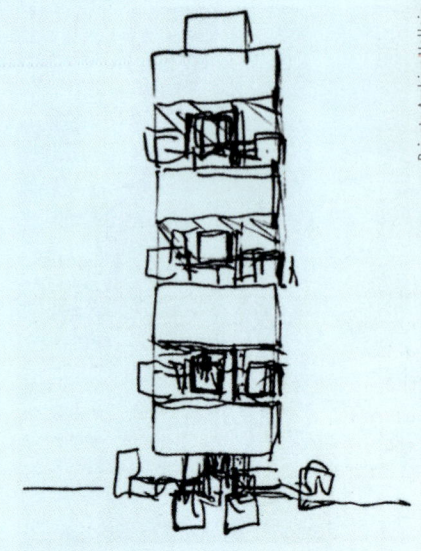

Private Archive Hollein

Commissioned by the duo of Southern and Bosera Funds back in 2010, the SBF Tower is based on an early sketch by Pritzker Prize winner Hans Hollein. It was designed to contrast the surrounding urban landscape and nearby skyscrapers as a recognisable architectural product. The building plan is square with 45-metre-long sides and 42 floors. The sculptural nature of the building is created by the alternating of six-storey blocks with linear curtain walls with five-storey terraced blocks. On those 'boxed levels', each floor is slightly different thanks to a complex matrix of deep setbacks, outreaching cantilevers, volumetric rotations, and subtractions. The vertical gardens integrated into the building contribute to increasing the quality of life of the workers as well as the environmental sustainability. Moreover, they undoubtedly generate a distinctive appearance.

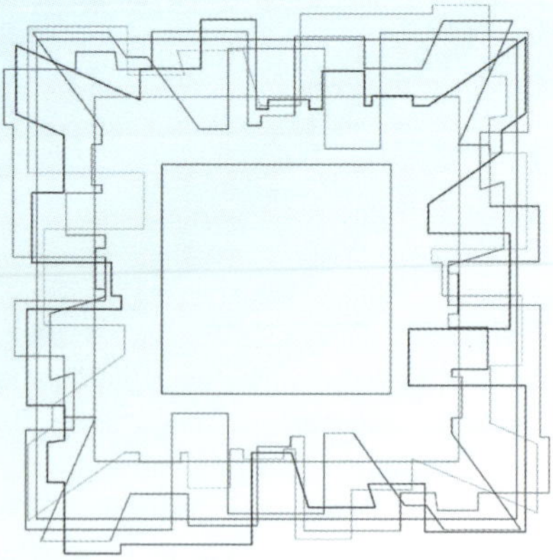

Christoph Monschein

Christoph Monschein

Shenzhen Stock Exchange

2012 Shennan Ave., Futian
OMA + Arup + SZAD
2006–2013

046 C

深圳证券交易所营运中心
福田区深南大道2012号

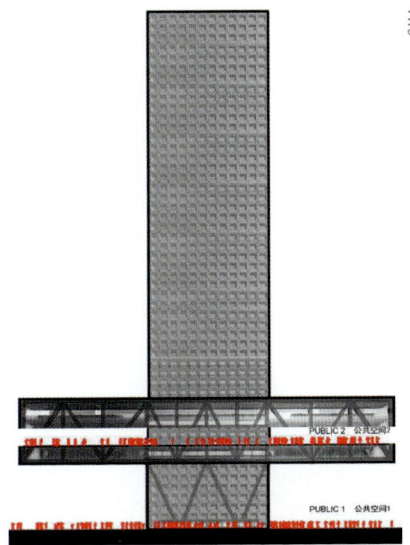

Breaking any typical architectural behaviour, OMA's design for the Shenzhen Stock Exchange is not an ordinary solid building standing on a solid base. Symbolising the financial concept behind the institution, 'the base, as if lifted by the same speculative euphoria that drives the market', floats above the ground. This raised podium is a three-storey cantilevered platform that contains the stock market offices and facilities. It creates a massive cover over the entrance and allows the ground level to be freed up for public gardens and circulation space. Above it, as well, is a large roof garden that increases the living quality and sustainability of the building; the building itself is 46 storeys high. The podium and the tower are both squared in plan and combined as one structure. In particular, the horizontal platform is framed by a three-dimensional array of full-depth steel transfer trusses, visible on the exterior, supported by the columns framing the atrium and tower. The 'deep façades' have a patterned glass cladding that contributes to reducing energy consumption and changes its translucency with weather conditions and night lights. The sobriety of forms 'obediently blends in' with its surroundings. Nevertheless, the peculiar profile renders the building both mysterious and iconic.

Christoph Monschein

Chao Zhang

Archivio Fuksas

it reveals the vertical fragmentation of the tower into three blocks kept together along with a three-dimensional void. This inner space creates a vertical tension all along the height of the tower and acts as a public space, interconnecting floors and condensing 'streams of light, images, and activity'.

Guosen Securities Tower ⌃
Fuhua Rd., Futian
Massimiliano & Doriana Fuksas
2021

047 C

国信金融大厦
福田区福华路

Line 1,3
Shopping Park
购物公园
200 m

Wuzhou Guest House ⤵
6001 Shennan Ave., Futian
SUIADR
1997

048 C

五洲宾馆
福田区深南大道6001号

Line 2,3,11
Futian
福田
550 m

Filling one of the very last vacant plots in the Futian CBD, the Guosen Securities Tower was the first tall ecological building completed in Shenzhen. Besides its innovative environmental features, the exterior is iconic thanks to a deep diagonal cut marking the glass façade. Thus,

On the western edge of the Futian CBD, at the corner between Shennan Avenue and Xinzhou Road, the Wuzhou Guest House occupies a corner plot of land from the Shenzhen Golf Club. An 'open arms' layout defines the symmetrical composition of the building and generates the front square; this square welcomes guests coming from all directions. The symmetrical composition of the building suggests a sober monumentality, recalling some traditional elements of classical architecture. The division into three blocks shapes the central one as higher and covered by a protruding curved roof, while the wings step back with large curved terraces. On the backside, the golf course provides a quiet natural scenography that counterbalances the high-speed road network bordering the front side of the hotel. All of these compositional elements undoubtedly interpret the traditional legacy of *fengshui* principles.

Shenzhen Special Zone Press Tower »   049 C

6008 Shennan Ave., Futian
SUIADR
1998

深圳特区报业大厦
福田区深南中路3018号

Philipp Meuser

Line 2,3,11
Futian
福田
1 km

Right in front of Wuzhou Guest House and overlooking the Shenzhen Golf Club, this publishing headquarters embodies the architectural image of 'news giant ship' and news observation eye. With a 260-metre-high spire, the tower is 47 storeys tall and has an elliptical plan. The basement has a boat shape, while, on the stem, the glass glaze wraps the exterior with oblique interruptions and a spheric conference hall protrudes from the façade. These elements make the exterior express a sense of freedom and movement, thus recalling the company's mission.

Philipp Meuser

C

SEZ Mid-West
Overseas Chinese Town

A former workers' dorm in OCT-LOFT

Enjoying the Outside World

D

Between the consolidated urban fabric of Futian in the east and Nanshan in the west, there's a seven-kilometre long area that was initially meant to buffer the major cores of urbanisation. Today, it attracts hundreds of millions of people every day thanks to its entertainment offerings and role as a commuting hub. In the early stage, green north-south belts were drafted to keep the natural corridors linking Shenzhen Bay to the mountain separating the SEZ from the outer territories of future development. Nanshan's sprawl was physically blocked by the Shahe Golf Club, a 1-×-4-kilometre strip of land along side the Dasha River that mounts directly in the bay. On the other side, Futian's growth has been intense but concentrated around the Central District, despite of some residential and tertiary settlements spotted around the fragmented green belt of the Mangrove Reserve, Shenzhen Gold Club, and Xiangmi Lake, with residual productive islands, which leave west Futian without a clear identity to this day.

This 'territory in between' is today dotted by the presence of the long-ago important rural communities that are still alive and recognisable in the 'villages within the city' of Yitian, Xiasha, Shatou, and Baishizhou; here, in the peculiar dense pattern of 'handshake buildings', is where most immigrants find affordable housing and a social network of assistance that is otherwise hard to find outside of these controversial informal settlements.

Since the 1990s, the core of this part of the SEZ was designated to the construction of an 'amusement citadel' where Shenzheners and tourists could pass their time spending money, enjoying life, improving their self-culture, and living out the blessings of the 'Shenzhen Dream'. This idea, indeed, moved the government and the state-owned company OCT to realise an extended archipelago of shopping malls and museums, like the He Xiangning Art Museum, OCT Art & Design Gallery (see p. 128) and OCT Design Museum (see p. 133) and theme parks like Happy Valley (see p. 126), Window of the World (see p. 127), and Splendid China (see p. 129), as well as unprecedented creative districts such as OCT-LOFT (see p. 130). It was the beginning of a new Chinese mass culture and of a whole nation's Westernisation of customs, starting from the city cradle of the Open Door Policy.

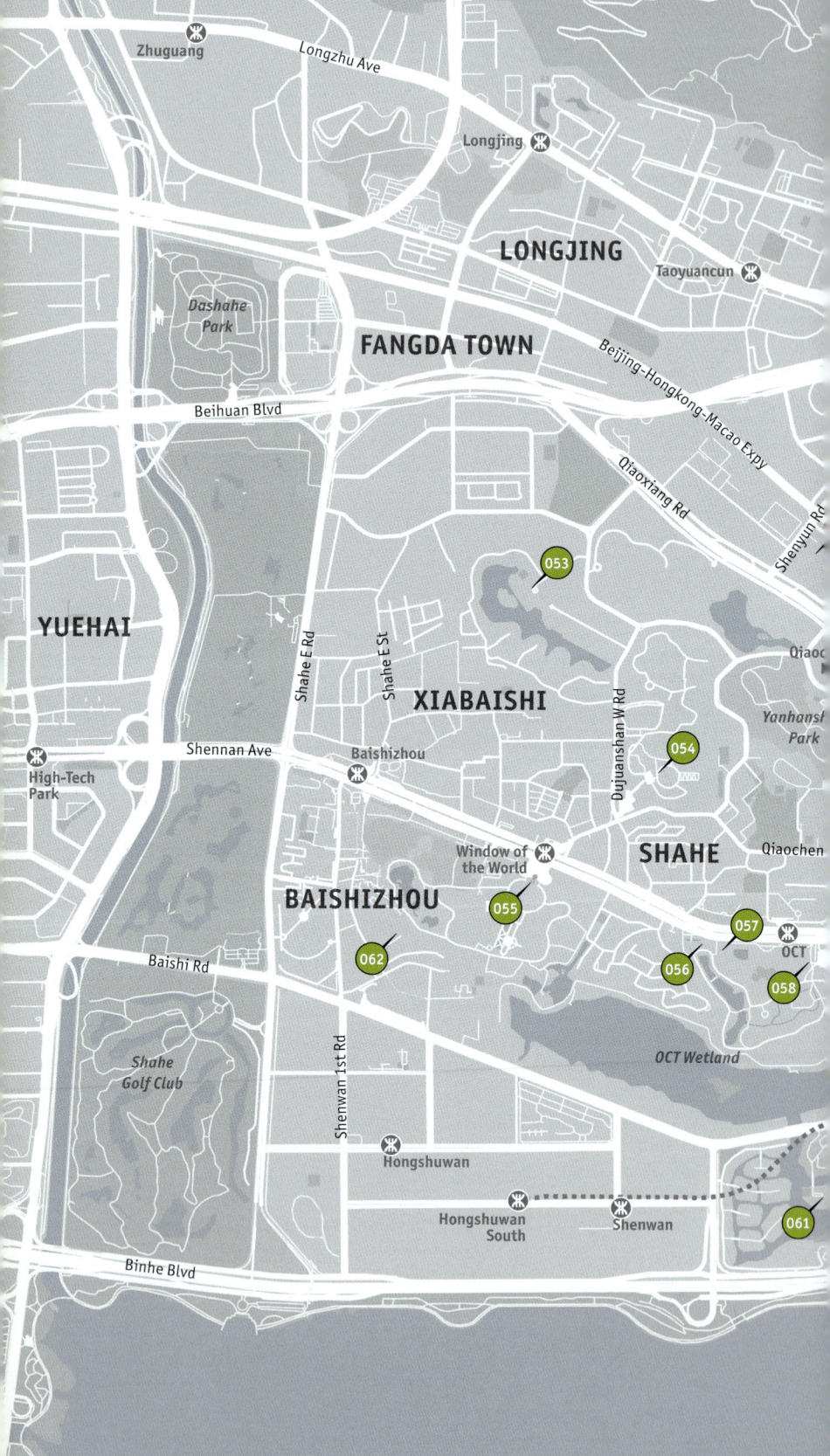

Zhuguang

Longzhu Ave

Longjing

LONGJING

Taoyuancun

Dashahe
Park

FANGDA TOWN

Beijing-Hongkong-Macao Expy

Beihuan Blvd

Qiaoxiang Rd

Shenyun Rd

053

YUEHAI

Shahe E Rd

Shahe E St

XIABAISHI

Dujuanshan W Rd

Qiaoc

Yanhansi
Park

High-Tech
Park

Shennan Ave

Baishizhou

054

SHAHE

Qiaochen

Window of
the World

055

BAISHIZHOU

057

056

OCT

058

062

Baishi Rd

Shahe
Golf Club

Shenwan 1st Rd

OCT Wetland

Hongshuwan

Hongshuwan
South

Shenwan

061

Binhe Blvd

Shenzhen Bay

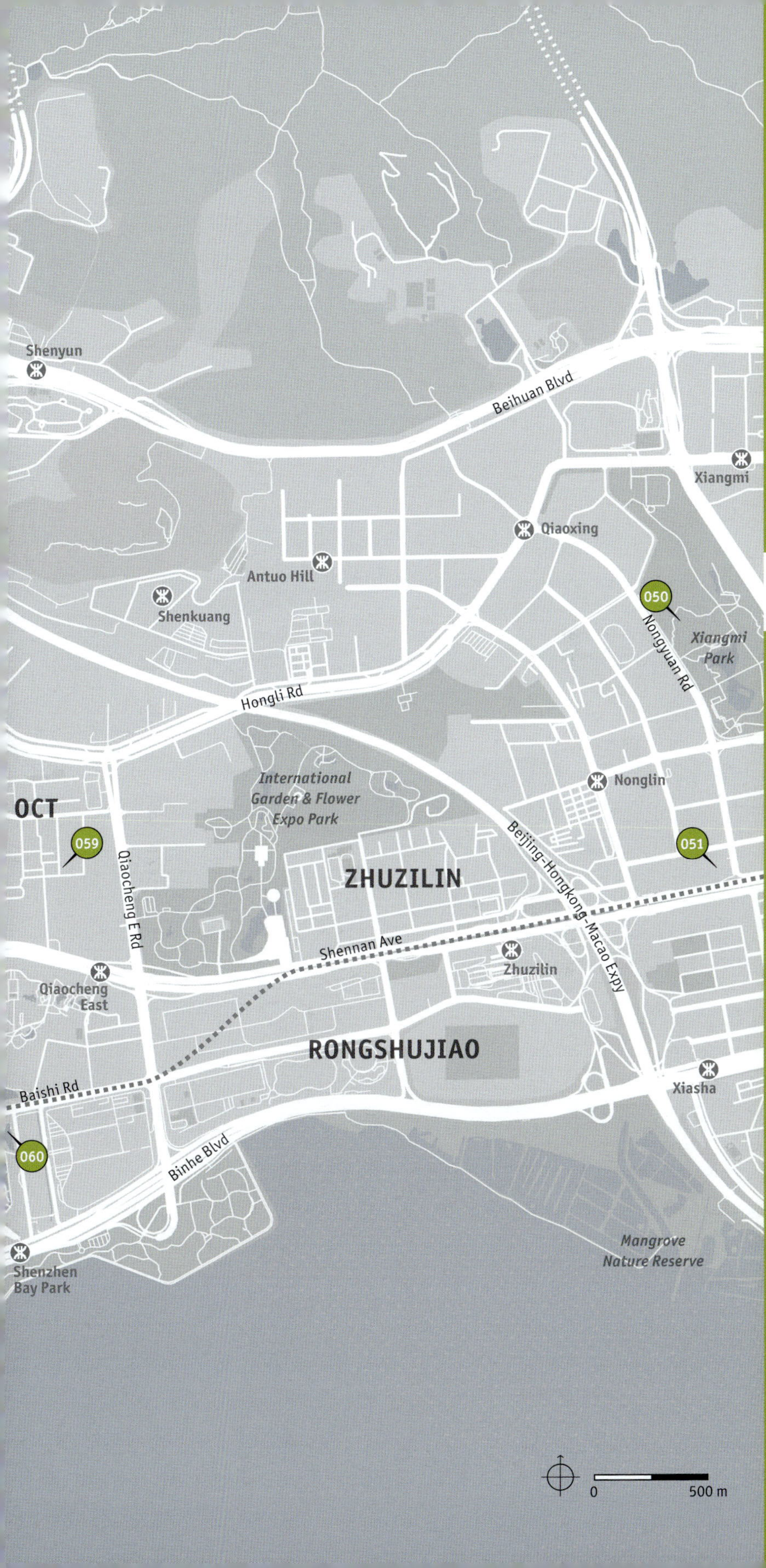

D

Shenyun

Beihuan Blvd

Xiangmi

Qiaoxing

050

Nongyuan Rd

Xiangmi Park

Antuo Hill

Shenkuang

Hongli Rd

Nonglin

International Garden & Flower Expo Park

OCT

059

Qiaocheng E Rd

ZHUZILIN

Beijing-Hongkong-Macao Expy

051

Shennan Ave

Zhuzilin

Qiaocheng East

RONGSHUJIAO

Xiasha

Baishi Rd

060

Binhe Blvd

Shenzhen Bay Park

Mangrove Nature Reserve

0   500 m

Vlad Feoktistov

Xiangmi Park Science Library 050 D

Xiangmi Park, 30 Nongyuan Rd., Futian
MLA+
2017

深圳香蜜公园科学图书馆
福田区农园路30号香蜜公园内

🚇 Line 1
Chegongmiao
🚶 车公庙站
1.4 km

Western Futian is a very green downtown area that acts as a buffer zone between the CBD and Nanshan District. Xiangmi Park was initially used as an agricultural research base until the quick extension of the city caused its decline. Intending to turn it into a public park featuring educational facilities, MLA+ decided to keep most of the pre-existing landscape layout, with its 40-year-old lychee orchard, palm tree avenues, and fish ponds, shaping a traditional southern Chinese park. Thus, they enriched it with new interaction with nature and, literally above all, a new pavilion-like library. It is designed as a contemporary interpretation of a multi-storey pagoda. The big metal cantilevers sunshade the glass façades of the inner box holding the education functions. The lightweight building is connected to a 'treetop walk' that snakes into the park.

D

Vlad Feoktistov

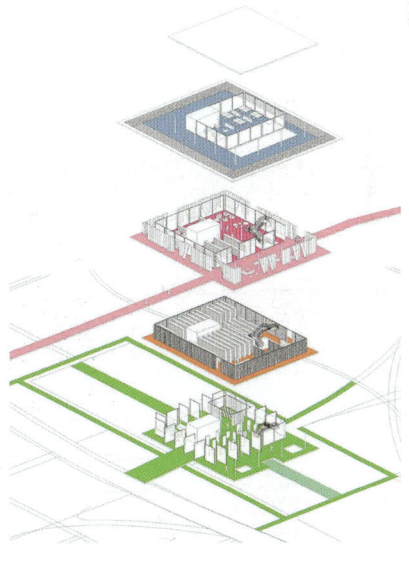

MLA+

Philipp Meuser

China Merchants Bank Tower (Marco Polo) «

7088 Shennan Ave., Futian
Lee/Timchula Architects + SZAD
2001

招商银行大厦
福田区深南大道7088

Line 1
Chegongmiao
车公庙站
500 m

The so-called Marco Polo building is a sculptural landmark designed by the same architect as the Futian Civic Centre. Its shape recalls the traditional 'doctor's hat' or a post-modernist version of a classical column. The building was conceived as an innovative steel-reinforced concrete structure with a central core for vertical distribution and a bluish glass curtain wall that covers the entire external surface. Squared at the base, its shape turns vertically into a regular octagon at the 49th floor. There, a three-storey-high sky garden is topped with a capital-like reversed pyramid trunk.

Wang Dayong

Artron Art Centre ⚘⚘»

19 Shenyun Rd., Nanshan
URBANUS
2015

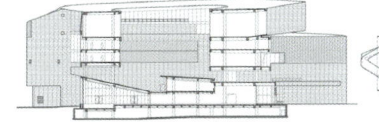

All drawings URBANUS

雅昌艺术中心
南山区深云路19号

Line 2
Qiaocheng North
侨城北站
1.1 km

Far from the main cultural route of the city centre, the Artron Art Centre is a one-stop comprehensive cultural printing service centre commissioned by the homonymous printing company. The triangular plan is conceived as a three-dimensional micro urban cluster. From the outside, the building is a blue curved volume between three highways, easily seen while moving quickly by. Inside, the library displays Artron's increasing book collection and others lay on multiple levels carved at the centre. Here, an open-air stepped court unveils the alternation of massive human scales that define this piece of architecture.

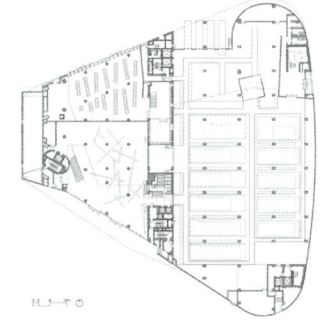

D

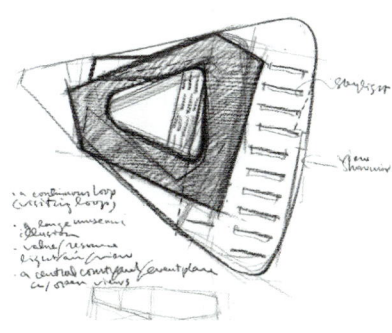

ZtpVision

there's nothing remotely similar to the original landscape replicated here. The presence of a central lake that recalls the Mediterranean seacoast is the only similarity to be found. At the same time, however, the rest of the space is a free interpretation of a generic Italian town, with promenades sided by trees, multi-coloured façades, arcades, and a classical-style clock tower that acts as the landmark of the public square. A variety of five-storey blocks, high-rise blocks, and single villas reproduce a microscopic town planned with some environmental quality. They are contemporary in design apart from a few decorative elements, which makes Portofino different from most *shanzhai* real estates.

Portofino ⌃   053 D

1 Xiangshan Middle St., Nanshan
Shenzhen Machinery Institute of Architectural Design + Huasen Architectural & Engineering
2002

波托菲诺纯水岸
南山区香山中街1号

Line 2
Qiaocheng North
侨城北站
2.1 km

As part of the OCT real estate developments in Nanshan, Portofino is named after the famous Italian coastal town, yet

Happy Valley ⌄    054 D

1 Qiaocheng W St., Nanshan
OCT
1998–2016

深圳欢乐谷
南山区侨城西街1号

Line 1,2
Window of the World
世界之窗
500 m

Walking distance from Portofino and other residential areas, Happy Valley is a conventional amusement park – à la Disneyland – divided into nine thematic areas with different exotic tastes, from

Philipp Meuser

Spanish to Arab, to Maya, to the Far-West. Despite being a touristic attraction, it is a intriguing place for those attracted by the architectural mimicry. A sense of displacement is guaranteed.

Window of the World `055` **D**

9028 Shennan Ave., Nanshan
OCT
1993

世界之窗
南山区深南大道9028号

🚇 Line 1,2
Window of the World
🚶 世界之窗
100 m

Window of the World was built in a time when tourism abroad was not far from being a mass-market industry. At the beginning, indeed, its purpose was to promote knowledge of foreign cultures and give people the chance to experience those famous venues known from books and television. Different from other real-world miniature parks, in this case, there are tens of famous historical sites, landscapes, and modern pieces of architecture located in an out-of-logic patchwork across time, space, and scale. A one-to-eight scale of the Eiffel Tower stands in the middle of the so-called World Plaza; an Italian-style maze surrounds a miniature Saint Peter's Basilica. The Sydney Opera House lays at the foot of Niagara Falls, next to a group of one-to-one dinosaurs; at the gate, a replica of the Louvre's glass pyramid covers the access to the metro station. Today, it is a true symbol of west Shenzhen. The kitsch atmosphere describes the attractiveness of this place, a node for people moving East to West along Shennan Avenue.

D

Qiang Jin

He Xiangning Art Museum ⌄ 056 D

9013 Shennan Ave., Nanshan
Lee & Lee Associates +
Sherman Kung
1995–1997

何香凝美术馆
南山区深南大道9013号

 **Line 1**
OCT
華僑城站
350 m

OCT Art & Design Gallery ⌃⚐ 057 D

9009-1 Shenzhen Ave., Nanshan
URBANUS
2008

华·美术馆
南山区深南大道9009-1号

Line 1
OCT
華僑城站
200 m

Named after the artist He Xiangning, this was the first museum built in the Shenzhen OCT area. With a floor area of over 5,000 square metres distributed between three storeys, the museum acts as an art research base with several artistic and academic programs aimed at promoting traditional and contemporary art. Inside and outside, the unadorned grey and white architecture expresses the sobriety and simplicity of He Xiangning's perspective on modernity.

Next to the He Xiangning Museum, the OCT Art & Design Gallery is the result of a rather remarkable industrial transformation. The building was originally a laundry facility linked to the hotel. Built in the 1980s, the warehouse was unaltered up to the early 2000s despite the rapid growth of the OCT area. The property owner envisioned the possibility of transforming it into an exhibition hall adjacent to an existing art gallery and URBANUS faced the difficult question of how the new intervention should relate to the existing 'urban leftovers'. Their main gesture was to wrap the warehouse with a grey glass curtain wall in a hive-like pattern in four sizes that creates an animated embroidery as a result. This theatrical dimension transcends the former spatiality of the building. Inside, this hexagonal form becomes a three-dimensional matrix shaping the interiors by using a variety of intersections and materials.

Je t'aime Dali

Splendid China Folk Village ⌄   058 D

9003 Shennan Ave., Nanshan
Meng Ta Cheang + Chen Shi Min
(Watson Architecture &
Engineering Consultants)
1991

锦绣中华民俗村
南山区深南大道9003号

Line 1
OCT
华侨城站
250 m

The pearl of all the Shenzhen touristic spots is undoubtedly the Splendid China theme park. It is the largest real-world miniature park in the world as it includes 1-to-15 scale replicas of 82 famous Chinese sites. The park also integrates the so-called Folk Culture Village into its fabric; this 'village' is an open-air museum featuring 24 villages of 21 different ethnic minorities. Beyond being a mere touristic destination, the interesting history behind the park is its philological accuracy. Indeed, more than 2,000 consultant historians, artisans, and engineers from all over the country participated in the conception of each piece of architecture and landscape reproduced within Splendid China. As a result, this park is considered to be a micro-atlas of China's vast and rich multiculturalism.

D

OCT-LOFT

Nanshan
URBANUS
2003–2020

059 D

华侨城创意文化园
深圳南山区

Line 1
Qiaocheng East
侨城东站
750 m

Nested among a middle-class residential area and the entertainment zone, the OCT-LOFT represents one of the earliest and most interesting examples of

industrial heritage regeneration accomplished in China. The site was a former manufacturing plant of the 1980s, composed of a dozen factory buildings, dormitories, and warehouses abandoned in the 1990s when industries left the Special Economic Zone under pressure from real estate. In 2003, the nearby He Xiangning Art Museum (see p. 128) set up a non-profit contemporary art centre, called OCAT, in one of these vacant factory halls, laying the foundational stone of the following regeneration. The firm URBANUS tested a new paradigm of

actions that could reactivate the area as a creative park with small-scale interventions, surgical improvements to infrastructure, and the active participation of stakeholders and in-house artists. Over the course of 10 years, the creative transformation was successful thanks to a sustained progression of artistic experimentation, general planning strategies, and space design conducted by the architects with the participation of the local creative community. The buildings were left rough and today are filled with art galleries, exhibition halls, studios, workshops, bookshops, cafés, and restaurants. The flexibility of the built fabric finds new aggregated logics, thanks to the open space design that sets new relationships between blocks by grafting and wrapping them at different levels. This character promotes a wide variety of uses of the space by diverse people all day long. Undoubtedly, the avant-garde atmosphere is truly unique.

D

Wu Qiwei

OCT-LOFT

Fang Zhenning

OCT Design Museum
8 Baishi Rd., Futian
Studio Pei-Zhu
2012

060 D

Studio Zhu-Pei

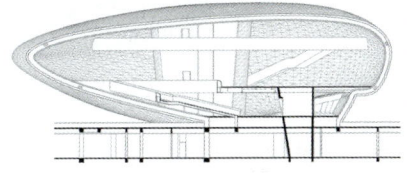

欢乐海岸创意展示中心
市福田区白石路8号

 Line 9
Shenzhen Bay Park
深圳湾公园站
400 m

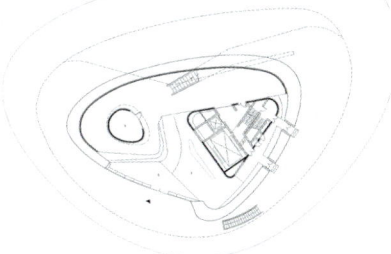

D

Not far from OCT-LOFT, the real estate company developed Happy Coast, a recreational area located on an artificial lake not far from Shenzhen Bay and Mangrove Reserve. The cantilevered kidney-shaped building seems to float in the air despite the force of gravity. It acts as an iconic landmark and its location on the corner of the site emphasises its attractiveness. The steel outer skin doesn't reflect nor match any other element of the surroundings. Moreover, the spaceship-like shape makes even the entrance hard to perceive and thus the whole building loses any sense of scale. This abstraction continues inside, where not a single standard wall appears in the absolute white bubble-like space. Only small triangular light holes let natural light filter in, creating a geometric pattern on the inner skin, which, in turn, recalls Le Corbusier's similarly poetic use of light.

Fang Zhenning

OCT Bay Clubhouse ⌃⌄　061 D

OCT Hua Forum, Nanshan
Richard Meier
2012

华侨城华论坛游泳池
南山区华侨城华论坛游泳池

Line 9
Shenzhen Bay Park
深圳湾公园站
1.4 km

Located on the artificial island in the middle of the OCT harbour lake, a crystal-like prismatic building stands like a rock on the edge of the water. The absence of windows on the entrance side preserves the privacy of the guests and complements the curved glass façade overlooking the lake at the south. The clubhouse features several recreational facilities for its members, like a restaurant, a fitness centre, a swimming pool, multi-purpose halls, and an outdoor sports field. Richard Meier applied his unmistakable palette here. The almost-seamless white Corian panels clad both the exterior and interiors, where shadows cast a dramatic play of light and darkness and intensify the pure indoor space.

Baishizhou Village ↗»　062 D

Baishizhou, Nanshan
Informal Settlement
1990s

白石洲
南山区白石街

Line 1
Baishizhou
白石洲站
1.2 km

Baishizhou is not a proper 'village within the city', although it has the largest agglomeration of handshake buildings in all of Shenzhen. It is composed of four native villages that once relied on farming, oyster raising, and fishing. The village occupies a long plot of land across Shennan Avenue, between the OCT entertainment area, the Shahe Golf Club, and fancy real estates. Inside the village, narrow alleys are inhabited by immigrants and white-collar workers who mostly work in

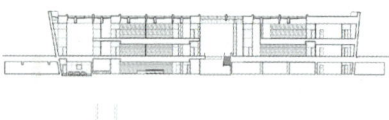
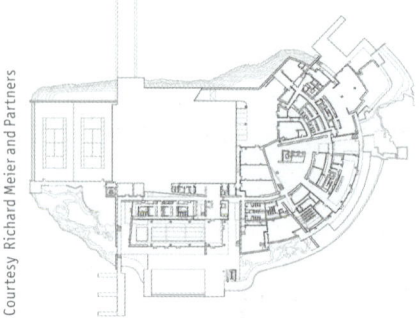

the nearby Nanshan High-Tech Park. The poor living conditions do not stop people from finding affordable accommodation in Baishizhou. In recent years, the village has attracted the attention of local artists and expats willing to help preserve it against the real estate pressure to demolish and rebuild the area, exploiting its market value. Thus, cultural activities have raised a shared consciousness about the role of people in the preservation of the already partially demolished village.

D

© Mapbox, © OpenStreetMap

Donghai International Apartment

051 **China Merchants Bank Tower**

A city view from Shenzhen Bay Coastal Park

041 **Ping'an International Finance Centre**

020 **SEG Plaza**

SEZ West
Nanshan, Nantou, Dachong, Houhai

Nantou Old Town (see p. 145)

Making Citizenship from Immigration

Despite looking less shiny than the other Special Economic Zone districts, Nanshan is considered the historical heart of Shenzhen. Xin'an County had its seat in Nantou Walled City, today known as Nantou Village (see p. 145), midway between Hong Kong and Canton. Oysters, salt, and pearls were the *yamen's* (local administration) primary goods. Until the Maoist era, waters lapped Nantou and the surrounding rural land. Then, with the reforms, Nanshan underwent a radical transformation and expansion thanks to the vast land reclamation that is still ongoing in Qianhai Bay.

As the early planners foresaw, Nanshan was devoted to higher education and technological research. Since the early 1980s, the Shenzhen University campus (see p. 152) represented a fine manifestation of the post-Maoist will to, first, make culture a priority in shaping citizenship and, second, to philosophically 'return to nature' through aesthetical landscaping of public spaces. Gardens, water ponds, flower beds, lychee orchards, palms, and many old trees together embellish Nanshan. This presence of nature has made the urban landscape more gentle than expected, despite the high-rise buildings that fill the panorama and overheat the streets where vendors sell food, kids play, and old ladies dance at sunset. The social life here seems more relaxed than elsewhere and district facilities, such as the Nanshan Library (see p. 148), demonstrate a rather sober aesthetic, mixing typological experimentation with modernist and post-modernist grammars and scale variations.

The residential character of Nanshan outlines a mixed pattern of urban villages, middle-class tower blocks, and student dorms, representing a complete atlas of housing types from the 1980s up to today. The same goes for malls and office blocks; few landmarks stand out of the massive series of buildings that fill the area, one next to the other. As the coastline was pushed further as reclamation land grew, space was made for new developments without necessarily needing to raze the early, extant estates. Since the 2000s, at the edge of the reclaimed land, mega-projects like the Bay Sports Centre (see p. 157) and the China Resources Tower (see p. 158) have become landmarks in post-reform Shenzhen.

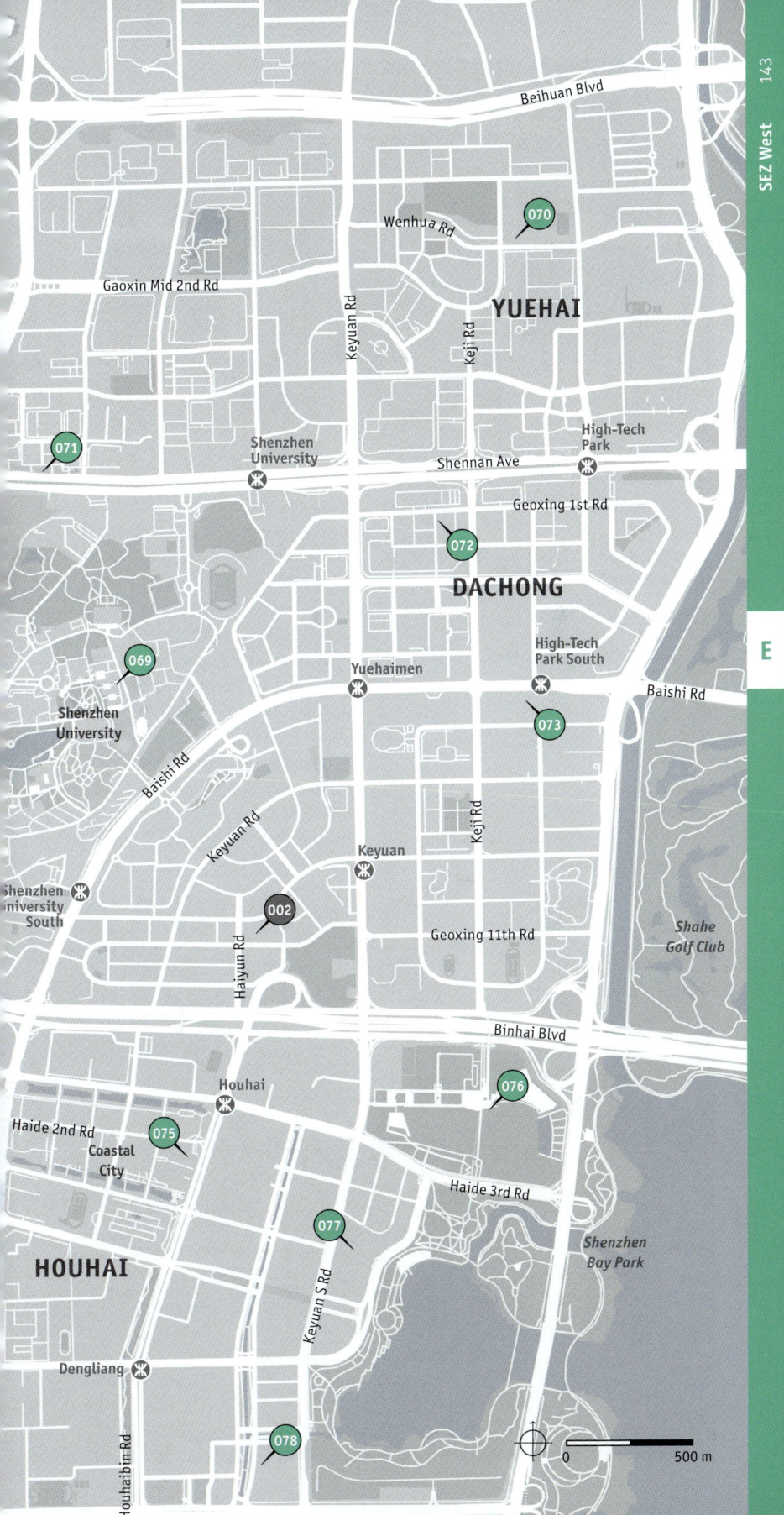

Beihuan Blvd

Wenhua Rd

070

Gaoxin Mid 2nd Rd

YUEHAI

Keyuan Rd

Keji Rd

High-Tech
Park

071

Shenzhen
University

Shennan Ave

Geoxing 1st Rd

E

072

DACHONG

069

Shenzhen
University

Yuehaimen

High-Tech
Park South

Baishi Rd

Baishi Rd

073

Keyuan Rd

Keyuan

Keji Rd

Shenzhen
University
South

002

Geoxing 11th Rd

Haiyun Rd

Shahe
Golf Club

Binhai Blvd

Houhai

076

Haide 2nd Rd

075

Coastal
City

Haide 3rd Rd

Shenzhen
Bay Park

077

HOUHAI

Keyuan S Rd

Dengliang

078

Houhaibin Rd

0   500 m

(sina.com.cn)

Zhengshi Ancestral Hall ≫

66 Nanmian W St., Guimiao Rd., Nanshan
Ancient
1800s

郑氏宗祠
南山区桂庙路向南村西街66

Line 11
Nanshan
南山站
600 m

`063` `E`

Located in the heart of Nanshan District, local villagers claim this to be the oldest ancestral hall in Shenzhen. Historians state that the hall was built by the Zheng family under the Ming Dynasty 700 years ago. It faces south and features three independent bays and a central door. Colourful ridges and brick carvings adorn the exteriors with mythological and natural subjects. All around the hall, a high-tech park has erased any traces of the original village, making space for office towers and residential high-density residences. Despite pressure by real estate to buy and dismantle the shrine, the local community and government are committed to its preservation as a symbol of Cantonese beliefs and respect for ancestors, and a shared symbol of cultural identity.

Nantou Old Town 🡖🡗

Intersection of Nanshan Ave. &
Shennan Ave., Nanshan
Ancient/Informal Settlement
1394

头古城 / 新安古城
南山区南山大道与深南大道交叉口

 **Line 1**
Taoyuan Rd.
🚶 桃园站
1.3 km

Nantou Old Town, also known as Xin'an,
is the remains of a walled city founded
in 1394 under the Ming dynasty that was
turned into a county-level seat from 1573
to 1953. Before then, it served as an administrative centre for the Cantonese
coastal areas, a trading hub, and a defence fortress at the mouth of the Pearl
River. The town is protected as a cultural
relic. The current boundaries correspond
exactly with the original ones: nearly 700
metres long from east to west and 500
metres from south to north. Traces of the
original road network are still visible, at
least in the central crossing axis that cuts
the town into four sectors. Along the pedestrian streets, several courtyard houses and ancestral halls have been preserved and turned into museums. The rest
were replaced over the years by the informal construction of the handshake buildings that have kept the town alive.

© Mapbox, © OpenStreetMap

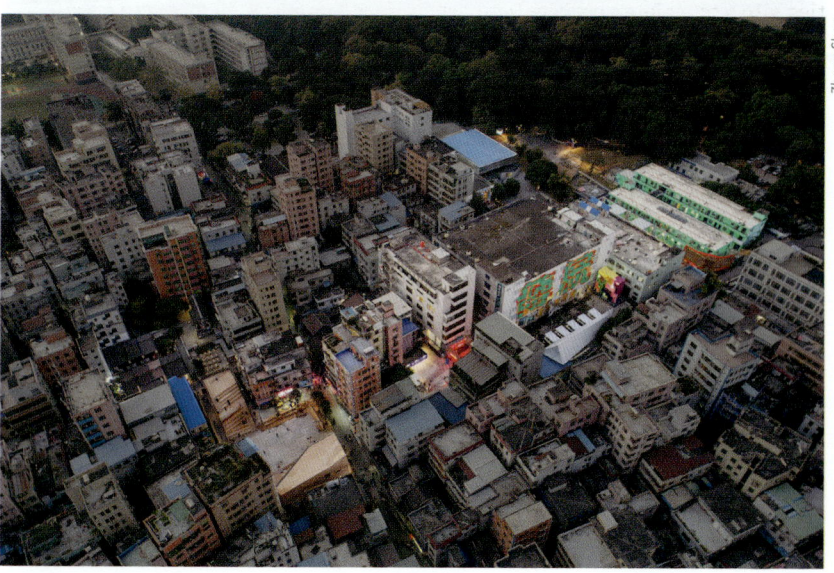

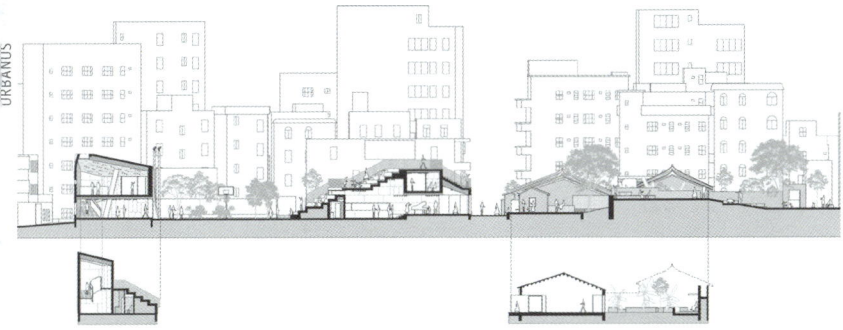

Nantou Old Town Preservation and Regeneration

065 **E**

Intersection of Nanshan Ave. & Shennan Ave., Nanshan
URBANUS
2017

南头古城
南山区南山大道与深南大道交叉口

In 2016, URBANUS's design and research team started working on a preservation program for Nantou Old Town. The firm concluded that only by respecting the authenticity of its history and cherishing the cultural layers and historical traces of each period can one shape a timelessly dynamic urban community rooted in local history and culture. URBANUS proposed an acupunctural approach so as to preserve the historical layering together with the cultural and spatial peculiarities of the town. The project aimed to rejuvenate the town through its cultural activities with a set of interventions on selected points which would eventually defined an exhibition route across Nantou. A few architectural additions condense into places for community gatherings and cultural activities. Additionally, urban art was implemented on several façades, creating a spatial narrative about the rise and fall of Chinese literature. This use of visual arts contributes to a smooth urban regeneration process that has improved the quality of life inside the village.

Guandi Temple ⌄

066 **E**

12022 Shennan Ave., Nanshan
Ancient (Community Project)
1612 (1997)

关帝庙
南山区深南大道12022号

The Guandi Temple was built in 1612 to worship General Guan Yu. The original building was a three-hall pavilion and it was rebuilt in 1997. The moon gate gives access to the ritual courtyard in front of the temple. Equestrian statues, figures of other deities, and incense cases adorn the building and illustrate the temple's role as an active place of local devotion.

Nanshan Library

176 Changxing Rd., Nantou,
Nanshan
Zong Hao Architects
1994–1997

067 **E**

南山区图书馆
南山区南头常兴路176号

 Line 1
Taoyuan Rd.
桃园站
650 m

With its circular plan and white cladding, the Nanshan Library stands out from the urban fabric that surrounds it. It is today part of a more comprehensive cultural cluster, together with the Nanshan Folk Museum and Nanshan Cultural and Sports Centre which were added later. The architectural result recalls some particularly American references, such as the works of Richard Meier. The building, indeed, is composed of two semi-circular five-storey blocks clad in white squared tile. The blocks are linked from one to the other by hanging walkways. They are also covered by a glass roof that is supported by a reticular steel structure. This cover generates a semi-open square – a sort of 'indoor-outdoor space' – well suited for the hot and wet local weather.

Nanshan Marriage Registration Centre

Changxing Rd. & Nantou St.,
Nanshan
URBANUS
2015

068 E

南山婚姻登记中心
南山区常兴路和南头街交汇处西南角

As Western habits have changed Chinese ones in many aspects of daily life, and marriage is one of them. To transform the typically unromantic governmental offices, URBANUS was asked to design a marriage registration centre that could become an appropriate scenery for a wedding moment and an architectural landmark for the local community of Nanshan. Designed as a small pavilion in Lijing Park, in front of Nanshan Library and not far from Nantou Old Village, it has a floor area of about 900-square-metre areas on two storeys. On the southern side, a pool reflects the building while a series of paths, covers, and ramps allow visitors and those attending ceremonies to walk, rest, and access the pavilion. The curved double-layer façade filters natural light, allows for relative privacy, and increases the emotional dimension.

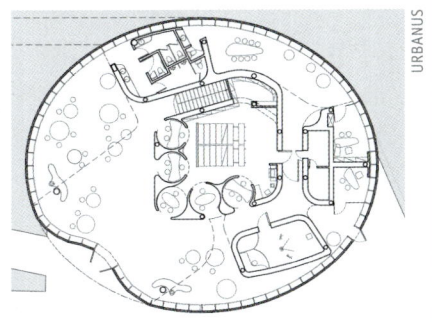

URBANUS

A students' dormitory at Shenzhen University

Shenzhen University Campus   069 E

3688 Nanhai Ave., Nanshan
SUIADR
1984

深圳大学
山区南海大道3688号

Line 1
Shenda
深大站
200 m

Already drafted within the first Shenzhen master plan in 1978, a land area of more than two square kilometres was planed for the construction of the Shenzhen University Campus, founded shortly after in 1983 and today known as 'Linhua Campus' because of the lychee forest covering the site. A tropical landscape designs the whole area where, up to recent years, numerous academic buildings have been built, covering a growing and diversified program from teaching, to dormitories, to kindergartens. The naturally sloping ground was landscaped to create a series of clusters organising the student life on the south and east sides of the campus and the academic venues in the central and north sectors. There, the old library is the physical and symbolical core of two monumental perspectives: one linking the library's western side to the main gate, the semi-open performing centre, and the administrative building; the other connecting the library's southern side to the Heaven Square, the new library, and the main teaching buildings.

Su Shengliang

Su Shengliang

Su Shengliang

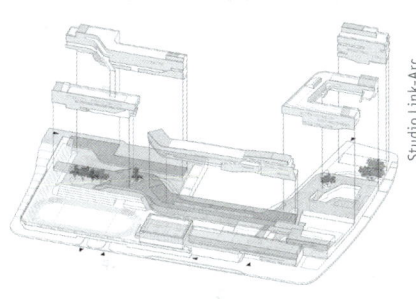

Nanshan Foreign Language School

070 E

2 Wenhua Rd., Nanshan
Studio Link-Arc
2019

深圳南山外国语学校科华学校
南山区文华路2号

Line 1
Hi-Tech Park
高新园站
1.5 km

E

Studio Link-Arc

Not far from Shenzhen University main campus, in Dachong neighbourhood, the Nanshan Foreign Language School is a private elementary and middle school, the last piece of a decade-long development of the area from an industrial outskirt to a dense vertical residential neighbourhood. The school campus is conceived as a vast horizontal garden, contrasting the verticality of the surrounding urban fabrics. A three-story linear block arranges the classroom along with the site, as architects state, 'chasing every available square inch of sunlight penetrating the surrounding concrete forest'. The grey-clad ribbon of classrooms creates a fluid sequence of outdoor places encountering the different educational specifics of the school, from enclosed open-air classes to sports fields. Besides responding to the school program, the variations in the layout were conceived to smartly react to environmental challenges, thus requiring weather protective systems, year-long optimised radiation, and heat control, to mention a few. These factors all contribute to the high architectural quality of the building.

Studio Link-Arc

02.2008

04.2011

04.2014

02.2017

08.2019

Tencent Building

071 E

10000 Shennan Ave., Nanshan
CCDI + B+H (interior)
2009

腾讯大厦
南山区深南大道10000号

 Line 1
Shenda
 深大站
950 m

ZTE Building

072 E

55 S Science and Technology Rd.,
Nanshan
AE Design + SEDI
1998

中兴通讯研发大厦
南山区科技南路55号

Line 1
Shenda
深大站
970 m

The Tencent headquarters is a true land-mark for Nanshan, located on Shennan Avenue and right in front of the university campus' open field. Although other skyscrapers now side it, this nearly 200-metre-high building features an unmistakable design, inspired by a space shuttle, with a convex rectangular profile that is entirely glass glazed. On the sides, the logo at the top mimics a gear hinge and signifies the position of the vertical structural cores of the building, which afford flexible interior space and well-ventilated elevator halls for vertical circulation. At the peak, a 20-metre-high sky hall reveals the beauty of the building's steel truss structure.

The ZTE Building is the research and design headquarters for the pioneer telecommunications company founded in Shenzhen in 1985. The tower stands in the middle of the low blocks of the early Nanshan High-Tech Park. Above the large basement, the tower is composed of two intersecting volumes: a soft-angled one that is triangular at the base and a cylindrical one that reaches to two-thirds of the height of the whole building. They stand out thanks to an elegant agave glass curtain wall alternating with horizontally striped, sand colour cladding on the corners and peak. The modern façade stands out from the flat surroundings.

ZtpVision

Shenzhen Centre For Design

B-Tech Twin Towers

Intersection of S Keji Rd. &
Baishi Rd., Nanshan
Tate Snyder Kimsey Architects
2018

073 E

湾科技生态园
南山区白石路与科技南八路交叉路口往

 **Line 2**
Keyuan
科苑站
580 m

Neptune Mansion

2225 Nanhai Ave., Nanshan
*Shenzhen Machinery Institute of
Architectural Design*
1994

074 E

海王大厦
南山区南海大道2225号

 **Line 9**
Nanshan Book City
南山书城
300 m

Located in the southern part of the Nanshan High-Technology Industrial Park, the B-Tech Twin Towers stand along Baishi Road and are easily recognisable for the peculiar folding effect of the glass glaze covering their side façades. The towers are 250 metres high and linked by a massive podium, so as to create a 'continuous ribbon connecting the horizontal to the vertical'. Beside the sober glass and steel exterior, the inner courtyards and a green roof surround the visitors with landscaped public spaces, providing a mixed program that is directly linked to the public transportation passing through the complex.

On a corner block next to the Nanhai Avenue Central Overpass, the Neptune Mansion, an office tower, acts as a landmark thanks to the gigantic bronze horses riding out of the façades. At 28 storeys high, the tower is paired with another 32-storey residential building located in the inner part of the plot. The office block has a triangular shape at the base, with three triangular steel-framed circulation towers at the corner and glass curtain walls on the three façades. Steel truss beams define the geometry of the exterior, recalling the post-modernistic juxtaposition of structures and cladding adorned by its special effects.

Poly Theatre ≫

Wenxin 5th Rd., Nanshan
Georges Hung + Huazhu
Architectural & Engineering
2008

保利文化广场
南山区文心五路

Line 2,11
Houhai
后海站
400 m

075 E

Located next to the Houhai metro station and at the eastern end of the Coastal City commercial zone, the Poly Theatre is part of the Nanshan Cultural Centre that was developed by the Poly Group. Motivated by the ambition to make the venue the most advanced and attractive in the city, Georges Hung designed it as a manifesto to his futuristic vision of architecture. Its smooth oval form is a strong counterpoint to the surrounding block-like commercial buildings. The greyish metal-and-glass skin covers a high-standard art theatre with sober and versatile interiors, suitable for opera plays and pop concerts. The Poly Theatre creates a strong connection with the surrounding urban plaza and helps give the Cultural Centre its sense of place.

Philipp Meuser

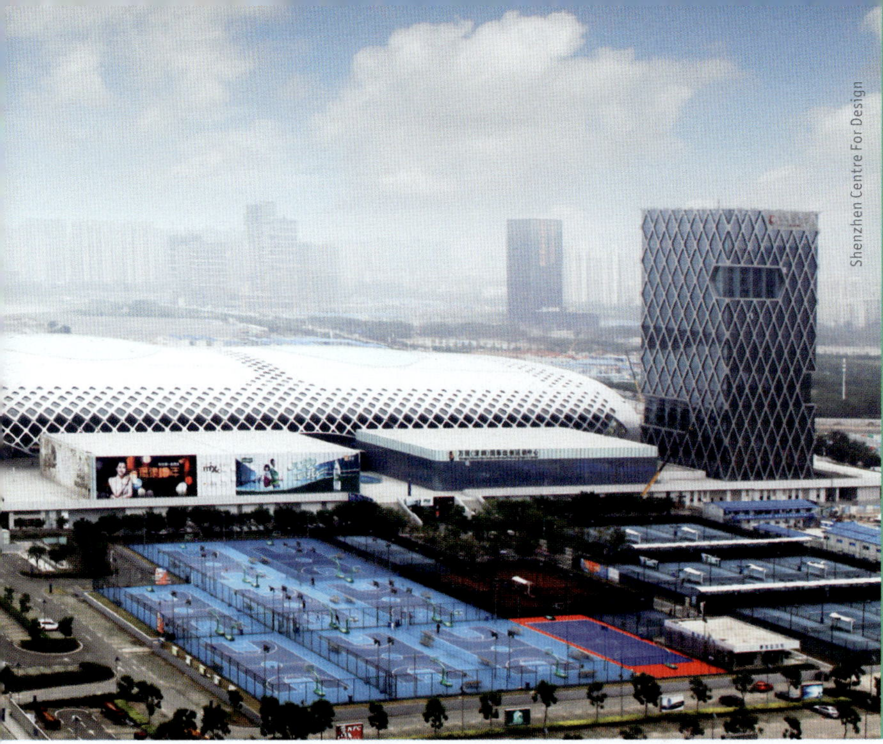

Shenzhen Centre For Design

Bay Sports Centre ≈≈

076 E

3001 Binhai Ave., Nanshan
AXS Satow + BIAD
2011

深圳湾体育中心
南山区滨海大道3001号

Line 2,11
Houhai
后海站
750 m

Nicknamed 'Spring Cocoon' for its organic shape, the Bay Sports Centre was built for the occasion of the 2011 Universiade, along with two other sports venues also located around Shenzhen. This venue is the most central one, located on a reclaimed plot on the north-west corner of the Shenzhen Bay, right near Houhai District, the OCT venues, and the university campus. The centre has a snake-like horizontal shape that stretches more than 700 metres long from east to west and 400 metres wide. The venue hosts an open-air football field, plus a swimming pool and a table tennis area in its covered section. In addition to the gigantic size, which makes it recognisable from a long distance, another peculiarity is the white alveolar grid-like steel coating that covers the whole building as a unique, sinuous skin.

wanghongliu (Wikicommons - CC BY-SA 4.0)

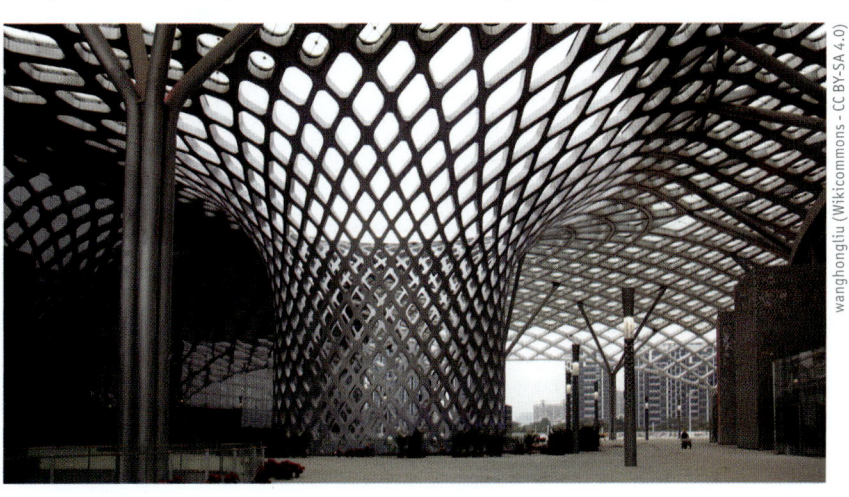

078 One Bay Shenzhen

Nanshan Mount

Shenzhen Bay Park Lianhuashan

A bird's-eye view of Huohai and the Shenzhen Bay Park

China Resources Tower

2666 Keyuan S Rd., Nanshan
*Kohn Pedersen Fox Associates +
CCDI*
2014–2018

077 E

中国华润大厦
南山区科苑南路2666号

Line 2,11
Houhai
后海站
1 km

This tower changed the skyline of the rapidly growing Houhai District. Inspired by a spring bamboo shoot, it has a tapered form with a circular base. Held up by a robust diagrid system, the building's vertical convexity makes the stem's 56 columns converge into 28 more massive ones at the top and bottom. They merge into a single point where a conical sky lounge allows visitors to admire the landscape.

Xinhua

075 **Poly Theatre**

077 **China Resources Tower**

076 **Bay Sports Centre**

E

Shenzhen Bay

One Shenzhen Bay ⌃
3008 Zhongxin Rd., Nanshan
Kohn Pedersen Fox Associates +
CCDI + AUBE
2014–2018

078 **E**

深圳湾一号
南山区中心路3008

✕ Line 2
Dengliang
🚶 登良站
800 m

Facing the Shenzhen Bay Park lagoon,
the award-winning One Shenzhen Bay is
a mixed-use development that includes
six residential towers, an office tower,
and a landmark hotel tower. All different
in shapes and details, the eight buildings
are clad in low-iron glass with vertical fin
shades that create a unified architectural
language. The gardens provide a natural
filter in front of the sea.

SEZ South-West
Shekou, Chiwan

辛桂鹏

'Time is Money, Efficiency is Life'

F

At the very south of Nantou Peninsula, the coastline looks over Shenzhen Bay to the east, framed by the Shenzhen Bay Bridge (see p. 168) and the South China Sea's waters – not far from the point where they mix with the fresh waters of the Pearl River. Pirates, traders, and colonizers have all sailed along Nantou and Shekou for centuries, as it is a strategic outpost for the purposes of the Chinese navy's defence and trading operations. Famous for the millennial tradition of salt production, oyster farming, and fishing, the original communities used to live on boats until the Maoists created fishing brigades with living quarters and low-tech manufacturing facilities on land. Despite the productive and continuously transforming character of this part of Shenzhen, several monuments still narrate the past's glories, especially on Chiwan Hill, where the Chiwan Ancient Fort (see p. 177) and the Tianhou Temple (see p. 177) overlook the vast portscape. Indeed, the port represents the real soul of Shekou, the material *raison d'être* of this district.

Two years before the SEZ was founded in 1980, the China Merchants established the large compound that is the Shekou Industrial Park, reforming this rural fishing area into an urban zone that would soon attract investments and business from Hong Kong and abroad. Since then, Shekou and its bays have been wholly reshaped through the land reclamation that has further and further moved the coastline, making space for brand new real estate developments. Often people joke that buying a seafront apartment in Shekou is a waste of money, as it will last only until the next land reclamation comes about.

Many buildings remain from the first urbanisation of Shekou, although they have been repurposed and adapted to the district's leisure vocation. The most curious one is the Minghua liner, today surrounded by Sea World Plaza (see p. 173), a Western-style citadel of shops, clubs, and cultural venues attracting expats and locals for its seaside allure. Factories, like the Floating Glass Factory Silo (see p. 176), and the urban villages nestled around the area are examples of proto-capitalist attempts to shape Shenzhen's fortune, as described by its motto, 'Time is Money, Efficiency is Life'.

QIANHAI

Yihai

Qianhai
Park

Lychee
Orchards

Nany
W

Qianwan 3rd Rd

Yueliangwan Av

Mawan

Qingjing Rd

Xinghai Av

Railway
Park

093

Linhai Av

Liwan

Nanshan
Mountain

Yanshan Rd

S

Xiaonanshan
Park

082

087

Sea World

081

Gongye 2nd

Xinghai Av

Shaodi Rd

Chiwan 6th Rd

Chiwan

085

Shekou Port

088

092

CHIWAN

089

Zuopaitai Rd

090

091

Xinghai Av

Chiwan
Bay

South China
Sea

Nanshan
Book City

Houhai

Houhai Blvd

Keyuan S Rd

Shenzhen
Bay Park

Nanyou

Dengliang

深圳湾内湖

Houhaibin Rd

Dongbi Rd

Wanghai Rd

NANYOU

Houhai Av

Haiyue

Sihai
Park

Keyuan Rd

Shenzhen
Bay Port

Wanxia

SHEKOU

Nanshui Rd

Dongjiaotou

Wanghai Rd

080

Shenzhen Bay Bridge

F

Shenzhen Bay

0   700 m

View of Shekou's Sea World

F

辛桂鹏

Nanyou Culture Square ⌄

Dongbin Rd., Nanshan
*Design Institute of Chongqing
Construction Academy*
1994

南油文化广场
南山区东滨路

Line 9
Nanyou
南油站
950 m

Located in the high-density neighbourhood of Nanyou, between Nanshan and Shekou, the Nanyou Cultural Square can be considered a relic of the proto-capitalist public architecture realised in the early 1990s. The cultural program is modest but includes a recently renovated theatre, sports facilities, and a supermarket. From first sight, it appears to be an example of the extravagant melting pot of Western references put together without any philological reasoning. This postmodernist mix makes the building a unicum in Shenzhen and it has become an intriguing place to visit.

Shenzhen Bay Bridge ⌃

Shenzhen Bay, Nanshan
*SZAD + Arup, ATAL Engineering,
MVA, Guan Shanming Architects*
2003–2007

深圳灣公路大橋
山区南深圳湾

Line 2
Wanxia
湾厦站
1.8 km

Known as the Hong Kong-Shenzhen Western Corridor, the Shenzhen Bay Bridge is a 5.5-kilometres-long carriageway linking Shenzhen and the Hong Kong New Territories. Jointly implemented by the two cities, each government was responsible for the development of the portion on its territory, despite different rules and standards for each side. As if that were not enough, the phases of design and construction had been an environmental

Shenzhen Centre For Design

challenge due to the ecological complexity of spanning across the sensitive Deep Bay waters, where shellfish are bred. The bridge is composed of three concrete viaducts, one at each side and one in the middle, alternated by two cable-stayed bridges. Thanks to this infrastructure, the vehicular connection to Hong Kong was increased by bypassing the borders in Futian and Luohu. At each end, the border facilities consist of passenger terminals, offices, and car parks. The bridge is visible from each skyscraper that overlooks Shenzhen Bay.

China Merchants Tower »

1 Taizi Rd., Shekou, Nanshan
Skidmore, Owings & Merrill
2013

081 F

招商银行新时代支行
南山区蛇口区太子路1号

 Line 2
Sea World
海上世界站
600 m

China Merchants Tower is located on the western side of Shenzhen Bay. It is the pivotal element of Woods Park, a 15-hectare development that includes residential towers, retail, and other facilities. The bowed and tapered form makes the tower sculptural while providing some technical advantages as it 'allows lower floors to slope away from the sun, decreasing the solar radiation that strikes the exterior wall'. The exterior is characterised by notches that modify the

four sides of the plan to allow quadruple the number of corner units on each floor. The façades are clad with a low-emission glass curtain wall featuring a system of horizontal glass fins and vertical aluminium struts. This solution reduces solar gain and aesthetically acts to emphasise the tridimensional profile of the building. By night, the glass fins refract the artificial lights, illuminating the greyish stem and making the top of the tower shine as a gigantic beacon.

F

Tim Griffith / Courtesy SOM

Maillen Hotel and Apartments 082 F

Yanshan Rd., Shekou, Nanshan
URBANUS
2011

美伦公寓+酒店
南山区蛇口沿山路

Line 2
Sea World
海上世界站
650 m

Wu Qiwei

At the foot of Nanshan Mountain, the forest area has been mostly occupied by housing developments in a mix of high-density tower blocks and low-density villa-like clusters. In the middle of these nearly identical commercial compounds, URBANUS had the chance to experiment with a different residential solution: a hybrid combination of apartments to rent and a hotel, breaking the real estate cliché. The master plan consists of a unique double-comb building that frames the boundary of the site and divides the inner outdoor space into several sections. Instead of flattening the site, the ground level reproduces the natural slope of the hill, creating a variety of views and connections across blocks. In a similar fashion, the roof dialogues with the surrounding mountain landscape. The compositional fragmentation generates a sense of mystery, typical of traditional garden design. The ponds, courtyards, and gates reflect the ancient references through an array of material details.

Wu Qiwei

URBANUS

Wu Qiwei

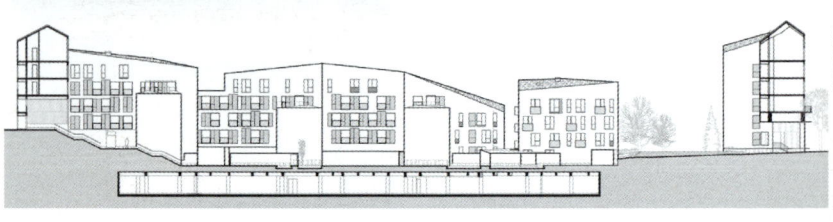

URBANUS

Nanhai Rose Garden

083 **F**

Wanghai Rd., Shekou, Nanshan
Huabaohong Industrial Company
2003

南海玫瑰花园
南山区望海路

✖ Line 2
Sea World
🚶 海上世界站
800 m

One of many seen around Shenzhen, the Nanhai Rose Garden is a prime example of a high-density housing development. Located on the waterfront of Shekou Bay, half of the site area was designed as a community garden, with ponds, pavilions, and some shared facilities connected to the ground floor of the residential blocks. The master plan consists of five-storey lower blocks that face the coastal promenade and ten 15-storey tower blocks. The long shape of the plot allows all of the blocks to enjoy the sea view while not overlapping in the typical choking closeness that characterises such high-density fabrics. Nevertheless, there is a typical use of elements that refer to Western decorative styles on the exterior of standardised buildings with no exceptional quality nor compositional innovation. Thus, steel-frame domains overhang the tower blocks and pink eaves frame their top floors, while arches and blue pitched roofs of the lower *dépendances* mimic some generic urban palaces from Europe.

F

Maki and Associates

Sea World Riverine Garden ⩗ `084` `F`

Wanghai Rd., Shekou, Nanshan
EDAW-AECOM
2011

女娲滨海公园
南山区望海路

Line 2
Sea World
海上世界站
600 m

As part of the Shekou development complex, the Sea World Riverine Garden occupies 2.5 hectares of reclaimed land along the coast. It was designed to achieve a set of sustainable goals, such as increasing pedestrian connectivity, providing a multi-functional open space for the local community, increasing the natural wildlife and biodiversity, and integrating water management systems.

Sea World Culture and Art Centre ⩘ `085` `F`

1187 Wanghai Rd., Shekou, Nanshan
Maki and Associates
2017

海上世界文化藝術中心
南山区望海路1187号

In 2011, Maki and Associates was invited to design a brand-new cultural centre as part of new Sea World development on the west side of the Riverine Garden. The building consists of a rectangular podium and three volumes extruded in the directions of the sea, the park, and the mountains. From the roof garden, visitors can perceive the natural landscape and all of Shekou's landmarks. Inside, the white multi-storey space is divided into a series of diverse places for cultural activities.

Zhang Xuetao

Sea World Plaza ⌃

Prince Rd., Shekou, Nanshan
Callison et al.
1984–2010

086 F

海上世界广场
南山区太子路

Despite the recent development of the coastal section around the Sea World area, the original core of this expat-friendly entertainment hub was the Sea World Plaza. The square stands in front of Minghua Ship, a luxury liner converted into a hotel in the 1980s, when the coastline wasn't yet moved as part of the land reclamation process. In 2003, the area was designed as a Mediterranean-style square with several low buildings featuring a chaotic series of references and strong colours. It became a popular spot for locals as well as foreigners living in Shenzhen; in fact, Shekou is still considered the most Western-like district of the city. In 2010, the complex went through a facelift along with an extension on the liner's southern side, adding new commercial venues and outdoor amenities.

Shekou Finance Centre ⌐

Prince Rd., Shekou, Nanshan
*Shenzhen Aoyi Construction
Engineering Design*
1986

087 F

金融中心
南山区太子路号

🚇 **Line 2**
Sea World
🚶 海上世界站
150 m

As one crosses the street between the former Sea World Plaza and the related metro station, this Brutalist skyscraper stands on a solid basement. It is the earliest and tallest modern office block built in Nanshan from the 1980s. Hexagonal at the base, the façade has vertical stripe windows framed by thin struts that create a black-and-white motif, contrasting the horizontality of the basement's bold curtain wall.

F

Shaonanshan

089 Shekou Cruise Terminal

Chiwan Port

088 Nanhai Hotel

090 Floating Glass Factory Silo

A bird's-eye view of Shekou

Nanhai Hotel

088 F

1177 Wanghai Rd., Shekou, Nanshan

Chen Shi Min (Watson Architecture & Engineering Consultants)

1982

南海酒店
南山区望海路1177号

Line 2
Shekou Port
蛇口港站
600 m

Nanhai Hotel was one of the very first hotels built in Shenzhen to host local and foreign entrepreneurs coming to town for business. Sensitive to the natural landscape that surrounds the site, architect Chen Shi Min designed a low-rise design with great attention to the environmental resources and site features. Backdropped with hills and facing the open sea, the Nanhai Hotel stays away from the city's heavy traffic. The building is composed of five rectangular blocks distributed along a curved line that echoes the edges of the seashore and the hills. The 10 storeys create a terraced profile on the southern side as each ascending floor is set further back, providing a strong visual continuity with the seafront, maximised natural light, and fresh air to the hotel

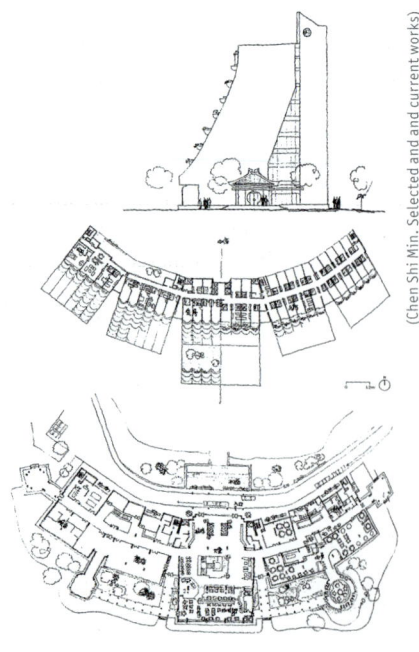

(Chen Shi Min. Selected and and current works)

081 **China Merchants Tower**

082 **Maillen Hotel & Apartments**

Nanshan

086 **Sea World Plaza**

085 **Sea World Culture and Art Centre**

rooms. The conceptual priority was to ensure harmony between the hotel and its
environment; the landscaping thus continues from outdoors to inside the lobby,
raised upon the site level so that visitors
could enjoy a full ocean view. Here, a multi-storey water pond and tropical vegetation create the impression of natural continuity across space and give access to
the basement floors where some common
facilities are located, so as to fully bene-
fit from the private gardens surrounding
the building. Chen Shi Min inserted several references from traditional decorative
elements, such as in the architectural design and the interior details. The building's fan shape is one of them, together
with curved roofs on the room balconies,
engraved parapets, and in-depth perspectives. In 2013, the hotel was bought
by the Hilton hospitality chain and went
through a partial renovation that altered
the original design, especially in terms of
interior finishings and shared facilities.

Shekou Cruise Terminal ⌄

089 F

Gangwan Ave., Shekou, Nanshan
Denis Laming
2014–2016

蛇口邮轮中心
南山区港湾大道

Line 2
Shekou Port
蛇口港站
1.5 km

F

Not far from Nanhai Hotel, the former
Shekou Ferry Terminal was closed in 2016
when the new, larger terminal was completed. It is now the principal passenger
terminal in Shenzhen. With a triangular
shape pointing toward the sea, the new
cruise terminal was designed by French
architect Denis Laming. Inspired by the
water's waves, the undulating roof covers the entire 12-storey cruise centre
and occupies an area of more than 40,000
square metres.

辛桂鹏

Floating Glass Factory Silo

Chiwan Rd., Shekou, Nanshan
O-office Architects et al.
2013

本次玻璃厂筒仓位
南山区海湾路

Line 2
Shekou Port
蛇口港站
1.4 km

For the occasion of the 2013 Shenzhen-Hong Kong 'Bi-City Architecture/Urbanism Biennale', the industrial sites around Shekou and Chiwan Ports became the location of several interventions for conservation and demonstrative installations. One of the most representative was the reconversion of the former Guangdong Floating Glass into an exhibition venue, as 'an experiment of rediscovering the lost spatial existence and experience via architectural study on contemporary industrial relics'. The silo building is 78 metres long and 16 metres high. It is composed of three blocks: two thin silos at the edges, four larger silos in the middle, and a block circulation tower. O-office Architects introduced a pathway inside the gigantic building and articulated the rough inner space by placing a series of transparent and opaque frames, walls, and staircases that could be reinstated at anytime. The curious thing is that the architects could not access the building during the design phase, so the project was conceived entirely on paper.

O-office

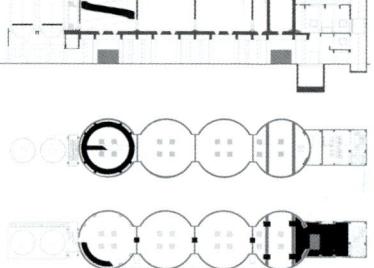

Maurer United

Maurer United

Maurer United

Yi Yuan Xinju (Wikicommons – CC BY-SA 3.0)

Chiwan Ancient Fort ⌄

091 F

Left Fort Rd., Shekou, Nanshan
Unknown
1669

赤湾左炮台
南山区蛇口左炮台路

Line 2,5
Chiwan
赤湾站
2 km

Reaching the top of Yingzui Mountain on Shekou Peninsula, the ancient Chiwan Fort still overlooks Chiwan Port, with its original angular bastion. This was an important defensive sea barrier against the invaders during the Opium Wars. From here, indeed, Guan Tianpei, the admiral of the Qing Army, defeated the British army in one of the many sea battles on Cantonese waters. The whole structure was built on large granite blocks where the left turret stands at an altitude of 170 metres. The site was restored in 1985, though the ancient barracks are still recognisable on the fort's lower levels and there is still a gun on the high platform to the south.

Tianhou Temple ⌃

092 F

9 Chiwan Sixth Rd., Nanshan
Unknown
1100–1300 BCE

天后宫
南山区赤湾六路9号

Line 2,5
Chiwan
赤湾站
700 m

Presumably built during the Southern Song Dynasty (1127–1279), the temple went through several expansions during the Ming and Qing dynasties; chronicles say there were dozens of pavilions, archways, sacred fields, and over 99 mountain gates. After two restoration campaigns in 1992 and 2010, it was eventually turned into the 'Chiwan Tianhou Palace' museum. It is located on the hills overlooking the Chiwan harbour at the southernmost tip of the Nantou Peninsula, a few hundred metres from the tomb of the Young Song Emperor (1278) – restored in 1911 by the Zhao family. Both are worth a visit.

辛桂麟

Tianhou Temple's roof

Yang Chaoying

Merchants Maritime and Logistics Tower

59 Linhai Ave., Chiwan, Nanshan
URBANUS
2007

093 **F**

招商海运大厦（海运中心）
南山区临海大道59号

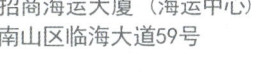 **Line 2,5**
Chiwan
赤湾站
900 m

the actual landscape surrounding the building is comprised of piles of coloured containers, sliding carts, and fast-moving cargo trucks.

URBANUS

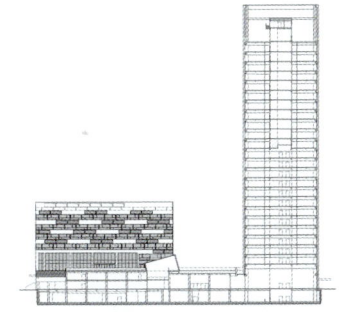

Located at the south-east corner of the container field on the westernmost side of Chiwan Port, the Merchants Maritime and Logistics Tower was built in a port area regularly exposed to the sea wind, several years before the reclamation of the nearby Qianhai development zone. Surrounded by large-scale factory buildings and piled-up containers, the tower was conceived as an oasis in the desert, aimed to act as a landmark visible to even the ships sailing on the Pearl River. The tower together with a second lower building form a dark-grey-clad, L-shaped complex that houses a document processing centre, offices on a lease, parking, and other shared facilities. Although the main façade, facing north, was enriched with flourishing vegetation and a water pond,

Yang Chaoying

G

Working Culture and Cultural Efforts

One could easily think that inconsistent settlements were present in Shenzhen before the establishment of the Special Economic Zone, but this belief is far from reality. Today Bao'an is one of most industrialised districts of the city, condensing some strategic facilities like the Bao'an Airport (see p. 192) – the third largest hub of Southern China – with the new exhibition centre that is under construction. A dense network of roadways connect Shenzhen to every point of the Pearl River area, an infinite system of productive plants that have mostly taken the place of the original countryside, and to brand-new residential communities serviced by efficient, eye-catching public facilities like Bao'an Stadium (see p. 188) and the Cultural Complex (see p. 189).

Despite its recent urbanisation, Bao'an County was founded in 331 CE, under the Eastern Jin Dynasty (317–420 CE). The location on the eastern shore of Pearl River Delta was crucial from the beginning as the waterways were the capillary networks connecting the coastal regions to the inner territories, crossed by rivers, creeks, and canals. Moreover, its position at the mouth of the river made the

Shenzhen coast the best place to defend against Japanese pirates and foreign navies during the bloody Opium Wars.

Over the centuries, indigenous people from the Baiyue ethnic group and Hakka immigrants have founded several market towns and rural villages where trades, fish farming, salt production, and agriculture contributed to the constitution of a wealthy community of clans who could indulge in literature, philosophy, and politics as historical chronicles report and as many historical buildings, like Qiyun Study Hall (see p. 191) and Fenghua Village (see p. 194), still testify today. The presence of a plentiful built heritage, well-preserved and nestled into the phlegmatic urban fabric like the Zeng Yaotian House (see p. 197), has recently moved the local government to undertake an architectural and urban restoration program that aims to not only preserve the material legacy of the past, but also to keep the shared culture of Bao'an's community alive, rediscovering a local identity through traditional architecture and folk customs. Thanks to the slowdown of urbanisation, the city has finally started rediscovering its own roots.

G

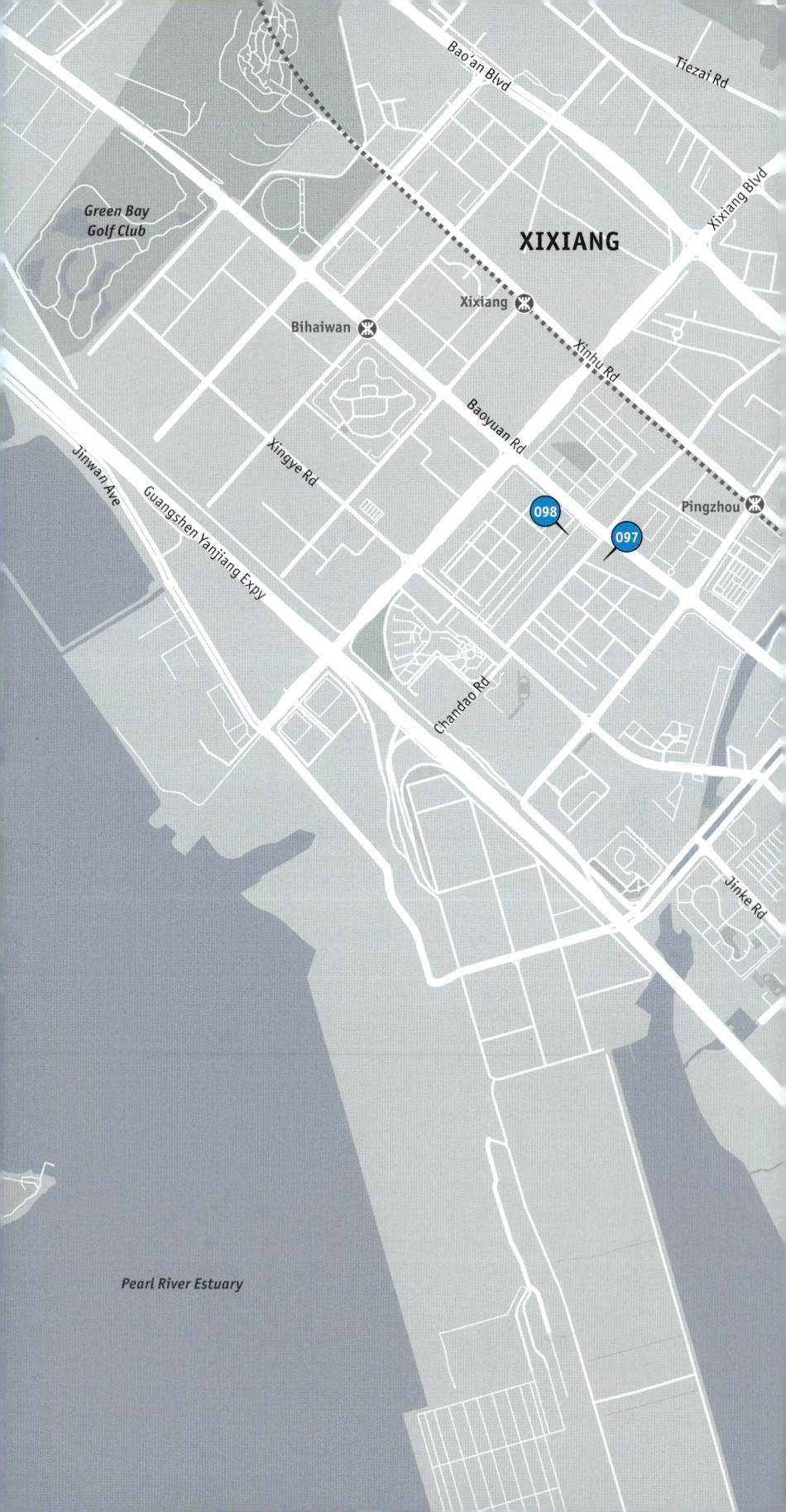

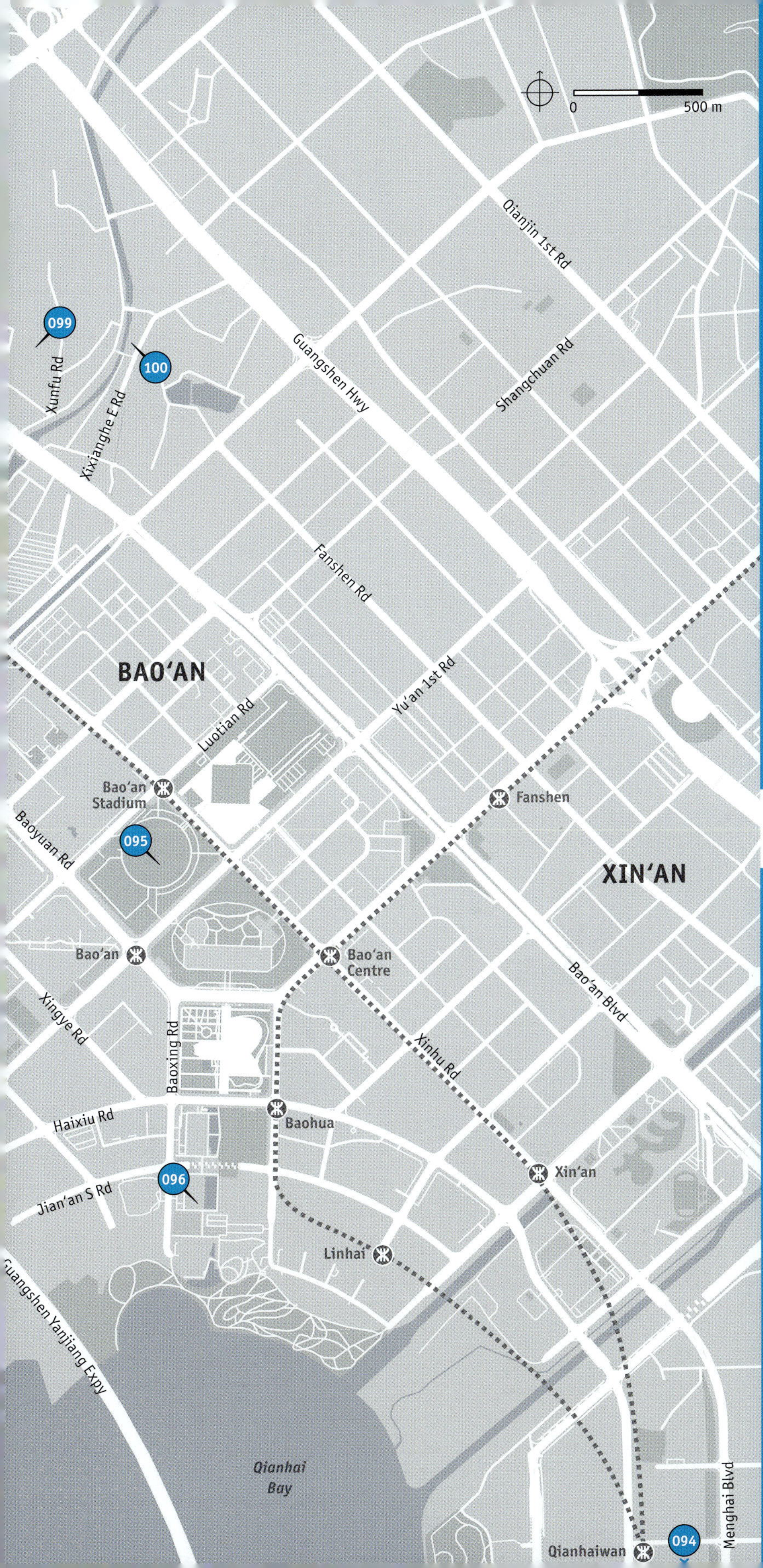

G

099
100

Qianjin 1st Rd

Shangchuan Rd

Guangshen Hwy

Xunfu Rd

Xixianghe E Rd

Fanshen Rd

Yu'an 1st Rd

BAO'AN

Luotian Rd

Bao'an
Stadium

095

Baoyuan Rd

Fanshen

XIN'AN

Bao'an

Bao'an
Centre

Bao'an Blvd

Xingye Rd

Baoxing Rd

Xinhu Rd

Haixiu Rd

Baohua

096

Xin'an

Jian'an S Rd

Linhai

Guangshen Yanjiang Expy

*Qianhai
Bay*

Menghai Blvd

Qianhaiwan

094

0   500 m

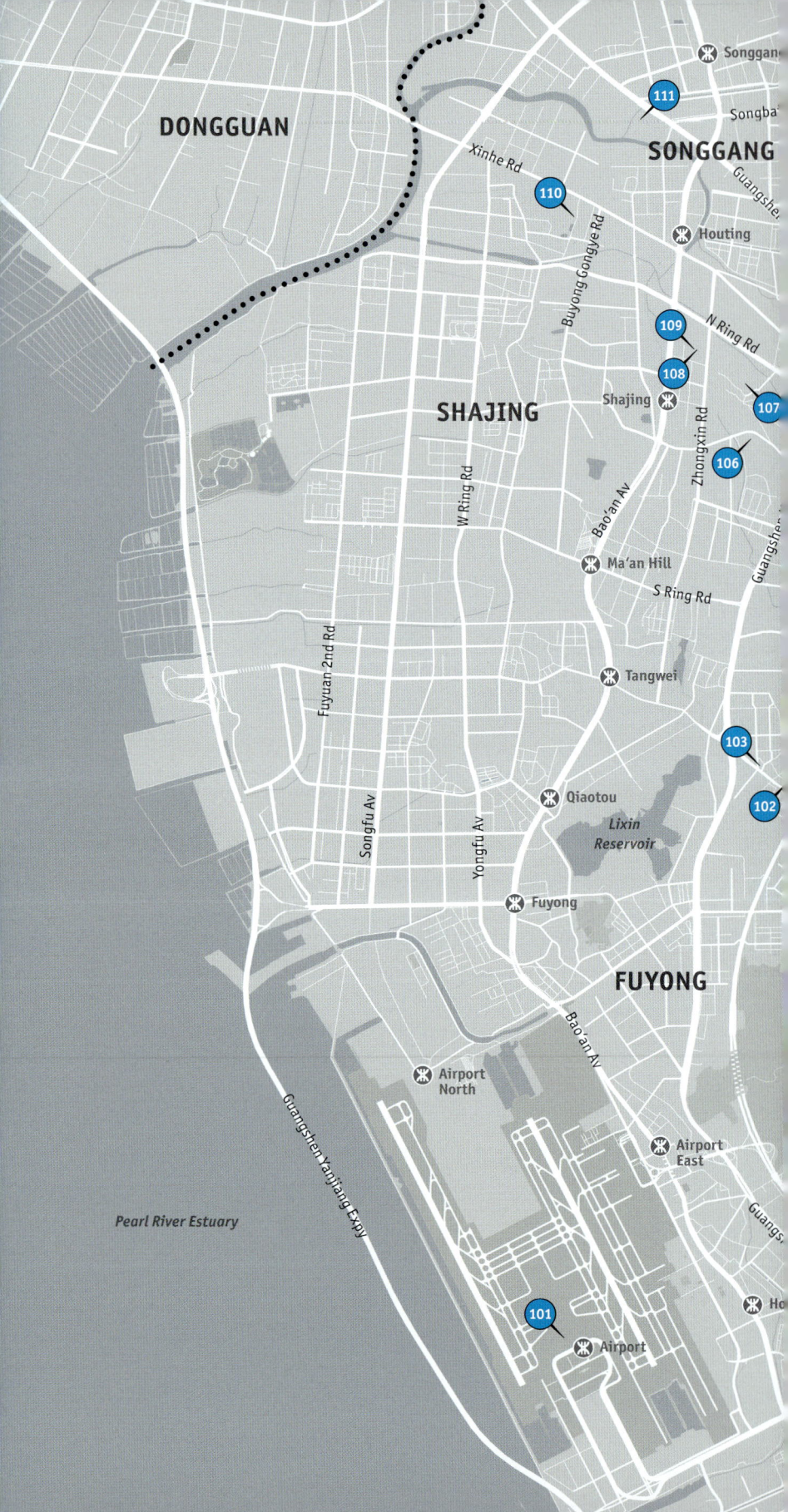

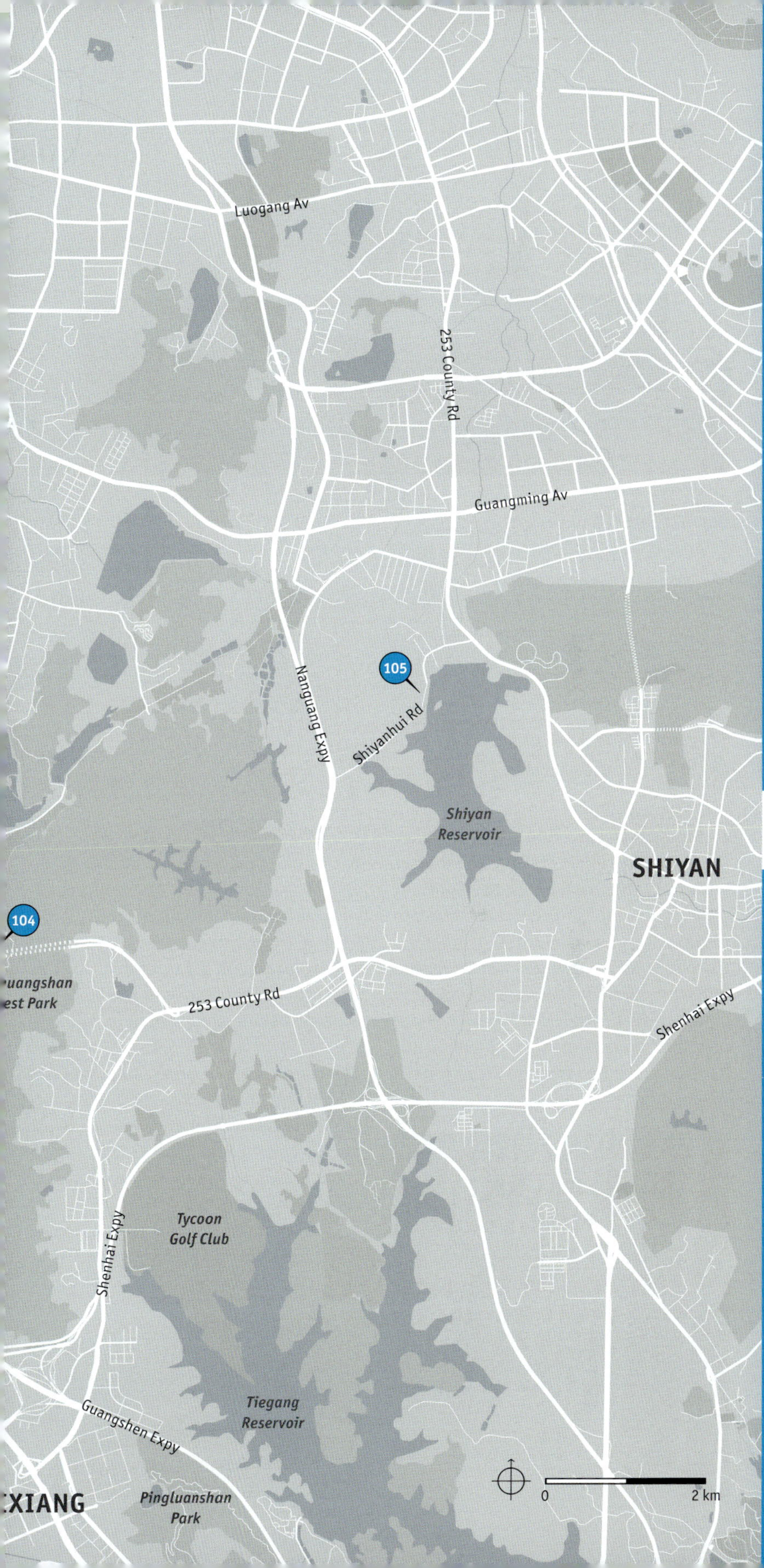

Luogang Av

253 County Rd

Guangming Av

105

Nanguang Expy

Shiyanhui Rd

Shiyan Reservoir

SHIYAN

104

uangshan est Park

253 County Rd

Shenhai Expy

Shenhai Expy

Tycoon Golf Club

Tiegang Reservoir

Guangshen Expy

XIANG

Pingluanshan Park

0   2 km

[Top photograph of the exhibition centre building]

Qianhai Exhibition Centre ≈ `094` `G`

Qianhai 1st Rd., Nanshan
URBANUS
2018

深圳前海展示厅
南山区前湾一路1号

Line 9
Linhai
怡海站
300 m

Located at the junction point between the former Nanshan coastline and the beginning of the Qianhai new development zone, this exhibition centre is meant to route visitors from the existing urban area to the new one under construction. URBANUS designed a building grafted on an existing one, both facing a water pond that reflects the transparent façade by night and intensifies the play between different materials and grades of opacity.

Bao'an Stadium ≈ `095` `G`

Baoxing Rd., Bao'an
gmp Architekten + SCUT, Siyu, SZAD
2011

深圳宝安体育场
宝安区新安街道卡罗社区裕安一路口

Line 1
Bao'an Stadium
宝安站
200 m

Bao'an Stadium was one of the sports venues realised for the 2011 Universiade when it hosted football matches. It is a field-and-track stadium for 40,000 spectators, located in a barycentric position on a square near Qianhai Bay. The design concept behind the stadium recalls the extensive bamboo forests of southern China. Two rows of green steel columns at different angles surround the concrete structure, supporting the undulating upper tier and the grandstands. With a maximum diameter of 230 metres, a tensile membrane covers the sitting area with a cantilevered structure of cable bundles, leaving the playing field uncovered.

Rocco Design Architects Associates

Bao'an Cultural Complex

Haitian Rd., Bao'an
Rocco Design Architects Associates
2020

深圳宝安文化综合体
宝安区宝兴路

Line 5
Baohua
宝华站
250 m

The Bao'an Cultural Complex is a cluster of public buildings that covers an area of 100,00 square metres overlooking Qianhai Bay. The project is the outcome of a competition won by Rocco Yim for a master plan that includes a library and a cultural centre, as well as a performing arts venue. The three buildings align on a central axis that extends from the inner city to the coastline; a series of outdoor squares connect them and act as a filter between them and the public park on the eastern side of the site. Although the inside of each building is designed according to its specific program, there is a unique architectural composition and coherent use of materials. Rocco Yim's work often hides quotation from the ancient cultural tradition, especially in the way he moulds the architectural objects and matter details. In this case, the three buildings' façades are designed as organic forms inspired by the Southern Chinese tradition of wood and ivory carving.

G

Rocco Design Architects Associates

Wade Zimmerman

Rocco Design Architects Associates

Idea Land F518 ⌃

097 G

1065 Baoyuan Rd., Bao'an
Zhang Miao Architects
2007

F518 时尚创意园
宝安区宝源路1065号

🚇 Line 1
   Pingzhou
🚶 坪洲站
   1 km

The F518 is a creative cultural hub, realised in 2006 as part of the Bao'an '11th Five-Year Plan'. The park was formerly the site of 21 old industrial plants, which were eventually transformed into a creative hub clustering several companies in the fields of fashion, communication, filming, and industrial design. It recalls

the well-known 798 Art Zone in Beijing and the OCT-LOFT in Nanshan district (see p. 130) with its town-like layout in which art pieces stand in the alleys and open public space between the blocks. A few buildings were added to the previous ones that still show the characters of the utilitarian architecture of early Shenzhen. Despite this, the intervention of Zhang Miao reshaped the general layout, public spaces, signage, architectural details, and new working units.

Avant-Garde Hotel ⌄

098 G

1069 Baoyuan Rd., Bao'an
Zhang Miao Architects
2013

深圳市前岸国际酒店
宝安区宝源路1069号

Right next to the F518, the creative park features a hospitality facility designed by Zhang Miao as well, the Avant-Garde Hotel. The name matches the architectural outcome of her design, as a statement of change, creativity, freedom, and opportunities. The pixelated composition of the façade is reminiscent of an integrated circuit board, quoting the futuristic vision of the F518 park. A look from the outside is recommended; unlike the exterior's strong character, the interiors indeed do not speak the same language, but are simultaneously ordinary and luxurious.

Wai 2012 (Wikicommons - CC BY-SA 3.0)

Shenzhen Pai

Xixiang Beidi Ancient Temple ⌄   100 G
24 Zhenshi St., Xixiang Town,
Bao'an
Vernacular
1573

西乡北帝古庙
宝安区西乡镇真理街24号

Line 1
Pingzhou
坪洲站
1.4 km

G

Qiyun Study Hall ⌃   099 G
80 Mingle E St., Bao'an
Vernacular
1885

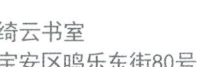

绮云书室
宝安区鸣乐东街80号

Line 1
Pingzhou
坪洲站
1.1 km

Not far from Qiyun Study Hall, this temple is dedicated to the 'Northern Zhenwu Xuantian God', a folk deity worshipped across the country. It is a tiny yet exquisite hall with a gate composed of red pillars and green-glazed tiled roofs. The open space in front is where the ritual dragon and lion dance has been set up on the third day of the third lunar month for the past 400 years.

This ancient building is the most extensive private library in Shenzhen, covering over 3,000 square metres. Founded by Zheng Yao, an educated member of the Zheng family, it is a dwelling with three pavilions and three courtyards. Protected since 1994, the decorative wood and stone carvings are outstanding samples of past craftsmanship. It is still in use, and cultural events often take place here.

Shenzhen Nanshan Ke

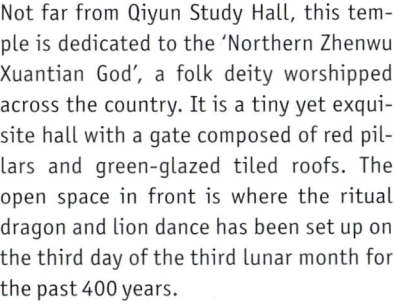

Bao'an International Airport T3 `101` `G`

Airport 8th Rd., Bao'an
*Massimiliano & Doriana Fuksas +
BIAD*
2013

深圳宝安国际机场T3 航站楼
宝安区空港八道

Line 11
Airport
机场站
150 m

Shenzhen Airport lays along the river coast of Bao'an. The first hub was eventually upgraded in 2013 when the third terminal was completed. Designed by the studio Fuksas, who won the international competition in 2008, the new airport is an approximately 1.5-kilometre-long tunnel shaped as an organic sculpture. As the architects stated, it 'evokes the image of a manta ray, a fish that breathes and changes its shape, undergoes variations, turns into a bird to celebrate the emotion and fantasy of a flight'. The conceptual image of the 'flying fish' was realised with a structural solution that was second to none in China and abroad for its newness and complexity. The whole building is wrapped in a double-layer shell made with honeycomb metal and glass panels of different sizes that can be partially opened and allowed light to filter inside. The curve shape of the casing increases the organic quality of the forms, making the roof and walls become a unique mesh. The roofing thus has a characteristic variation in height, recalling the natural landscape, dotted with irregular skylights that naturally let daylight through. This plasticity shapes the interior as well. Along the long 'tail' of the terminal, passengers feel like they are inside a fish belly, as this fully white space has a honeycomb skin on its ceiling that is reflected all over the glossy pavement flooring. The terminal program is arranged on multiple floors running below the main concourse. The vertical stratification of layers is

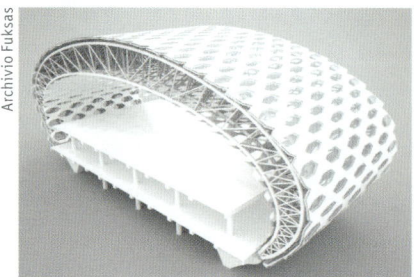

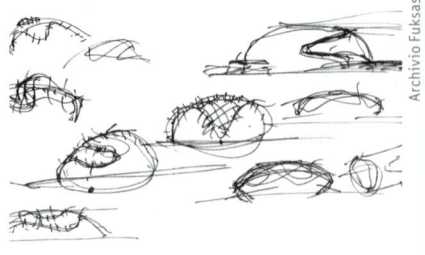

Archivio Fuksas

Archivio Fuksas

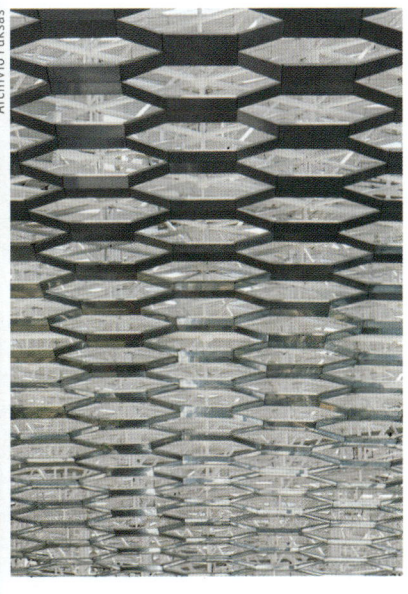

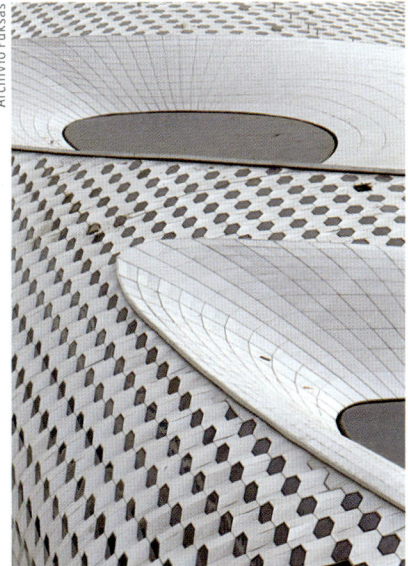

visible at three intersection points where the full height voids allow natural light to filter down to the waiting room at ground zero. Mechanical appliances are hidden behind the ceiling or, as in the case of the air conditioning, are shaped as big white stylised trees located along the 'tail'. This work is often perceived by observers as a light, free-standing building, despite the solid presence of V-shaped columns and tensile beams that support its complex structural system.

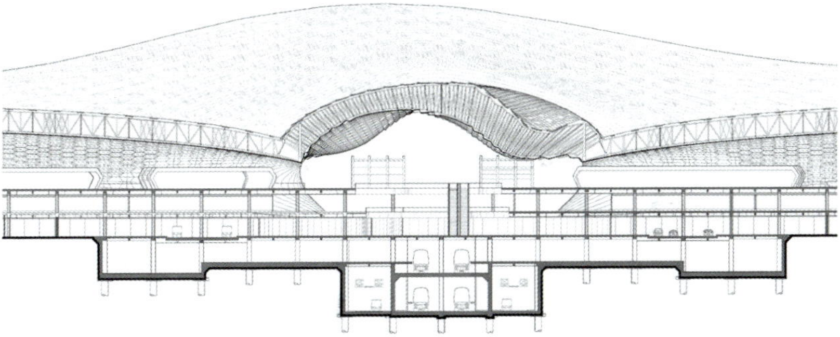

Archivio Fuksas

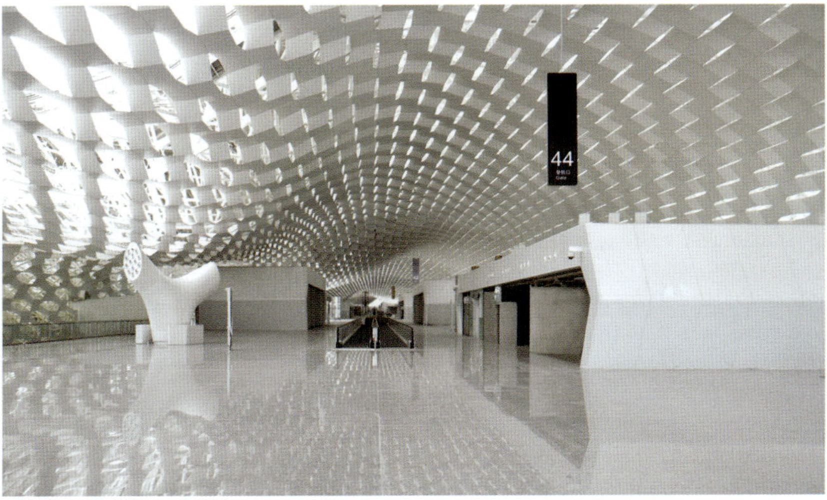

Archivio Fuksas

Fenghuang Village

Fenghuangshan Ave., Bao'an
Vernacular
1275 (late Song dynasty)

102 G

凤凰古村文
宝安区凤凰山大道

Line 11
Tangwei
塘尾站
3 km (Bus m252)

Near the airport, Fenghuang Village, also known as Lingxia or Phoenix Village, is the largest and best-preserved ancient settlement in Shenzhen. Archaeologists found evidence of human presence since the late Neolithic age, although the village was formally settled by Wen Tianxiang, a famous anti-Yuan hero in the late Southern Song Dynasty, in 1275. The Wen clan unified the urban layout of the village and its architecture according to the Cantonese style typical of Southern China. The 'comb layout' of the narrow streets organises rows of courtyard houses. An abundance of wood- and stone-carved figures and patterns decorate the buildings both inside and outside, revealing the rich symbolism linked to nature and the mastery of ancient artisans. Thanks to the city government's restoration completed in 2014, 69 Ming and Tang houses, 5 study rooms, and 12 shrines were restored together with the public spaces and nearly 40 alleys.

Shenzhen Centre For Design

G

辛桂鵬

Fenghuang Wenchang Tower » `103` `G`

198 Fenghuangshan Ave., Bao'an
Ancient
1816

凤凰文昌塔
宝安区凤凰山大道198号

Built under the Qing Dynasty, the Wenchang Tower is the highest ancient tower remaining in Shenzhen. Hexagonal at the base, it is 20 metres high and made with blue bricks. It is divided into six modules, from bigger to smaller in the plan up to the top. Each level is crowned by eaves made of five layers of rhomboid teeth and seven layers of flat bricks, while the spire stands vertically on top. A creek snakes around it, crossing the square shadowed by huge banyans. The pagoda is dedicated to Emperor Wenchang who, with Confucius, was often worshipped for the blessings of talent, wisdom, and erudition.

Fengyan Ancient Temple ≽

Fenghuang Village, Bao'an
Ancient (Community Project)
1300s (1983)

凤岩古庙
宝安区福永街道凤凰村凤

Line 11
Tangwei
塘尾站
2.7 km

The Fengyan Temple has a history of more than 600 years that is related to the legendary presence of Guanyin Bodhisattva on Phoenix Mountain and the feats of Wen Tianxiang – a famous anti-Yuan hero who founded Fenghuang Village – and his ancestors. The religious compound is part of Fenghuang Mountain Scenic Area, a natural reservoir surrounded by mountains on three sides and facing the sea on the other. Located halfway from the peak, the temple's mountain background feels protective. From the temple, fairy-tale paths go deep inside the forest where strands, arches, and carved stones mark the route up the mountain. It was rebuilt many times during the Ming, Qing, and Republic of China eras, and was eventually annihilated for more than 30 years, during the Maoist period. In 1983, the descendants of Lingxia Village funded the latest reconstruction to include new facilities for devotees and tourists. The pavilions recall the traditional language of ancient architectural styles, though they are new and made with non-traditional techniques. This site is worth the journey.

Hongyuan Temple ≽

85 Xinghu Rd., Bao'an
Ancient
1800s

弘源寺
宝安区星湖路85号

Line 11
Houting
后亭站
12.5 km (Bus m442)

Built during the late Qing Dynasty, not far from the Fengyan Temple, the Hongyuan Temple was initially known as the Wushi Temple. It was destroyed and repaired several times before the last restoration in 1999. The complex stands in the middle of the mountain, with an elegant, monastic allure. There are three halls and six bell towers, one on each side of each hall, arranged symmetrically up the slope.

Shenzhen Centre For Design

G

Zeng Yaotian House

106 G

149 Xinsha Rd., Shangxing
Community, Shajing St., Bao'an
Unknown
Early 1900s

曾耀添宅
宝安区沙井街道上星社区新沙路149号

Line 11
Qiaotou
桥头站
1 km

The Zeng Yaotian House is one of the very few *dialous* visible in Shenzhen, a relative of the most famous ones in Kaiping. It was built by Zeng Shi, a native to this area who moved abroad and eventually returned; he financed the construction of such a building to ensure the security of his family members who had remained in China. The house was the tallest building in Shangxing at the time and, like the ones in Kaiping, it used to be a multi-storey watchtower for defence. Indeed, the ground floor has one entrance and originally no windows, in order to deter forays by bandits. The upper floor used to serve as living quarters where the abundance of openings denote the residential function of the building. Featuring a mix of Chinese and Western architectural elements, the structure is concrete, and the upper floors are framed by cantilevered Roman-style arcades, topped by a domed pavilion on the rooftop. The eclectic combination of Western-style decorations is counterbalanced by a traditional residential layout with an inner courtyard and rooms arranged around it. Today, several households inhabit the house. Thanks to its uniqueness, it has been protected and conserved as a cultural relic by the local government since 2003.

Yongxing Bridge

Zeng's Grand Ancestral Hall ⌄  107 G

Shenxiang Rd., Bao'an
Vernacular
1798

曾氏大宗祠
宝安区深巷路

 Line 11
Houting
后亭站
2.5 km (Bus m442)

Xinqiao Village became the hometown of the Zengs after they moved southward to Bao'an. Here, the clan's ancestral hall was built during the Qianlong period of the Qing Dynasty (1735–1795) and expanded in 1798. Restored in 2005, the shrine is a Guangfu building with three entrances and five halls, 20 metres wide by 50 metres deep. The front, central, back halls are interspersed by courtyards that give

access to the left and right pavilions and minor rooms. The overall decoration combines stone carving, wood carving, mural painting, grey plaster, brick carving, and porcelain details with a bright combination of blues, reds, and greens.

Guang'an Ancient Pawnshop ↗ 108 G

Qiaotou N Rd., Bao'an
Ancient
1800s

广安当铺
宝安区桥头北路

 Line 11
Shajing
沙井站
1.3 km

In the middle of Xinqiao Village, the tallest ancient building standing is the Guang'an Pawnshop. Built by an overseas Chinese in the United States of America, for over a century it was the largest pawnshop in Shenzhen and its environs. The building is composed of a tower block, two annex buildings, a courtyard, and gate building. The main one is a six-storey square turret-style block, with straight edges, tiny windows, and a terrace roof. Today it is relatively well-preserved; on the outer walls, countless bullet holes trace a long history of robberies.

Shenzhen Centre For Design

Shenzhen Centre for Design

Yongxing Bridge ⌄

Qiaotou N Rd., Bao'an
Ancient
1785

109 G

永兴桥
宝安区桥头北路

Right next to the Ancient Pawnshop, the Maozhou River flows across the neighbourhood and it is the Yongxing Bridge that connects the two sides of the river banks. The bridge was originally a wooden structure built by the superintendent Zeng Qiaochuan during the Kangxi period (1622–1722) of the Qing Dynasty. Later on, however, the wooden bridge was replaced by a stone one which was donated by the Zeng clan. Still used today by pedestrians, the bridge is a three-hole squat stone arch with a length of 50 metres and a width of 3.5 metres. The biggest hole is five metres high, suitable for small boats to transit through. The bridge is made of granite stone blocks and the railing is decorated with embossed dragon and phoenix patterns as well as stone lions. Unique in its kind in Shenzhen, the Yongxing Bridge is still intact, despite decades of careless use.

G

辛桂鹏

Jiang's Grand Shrine ⌄  `110` `G`
SW intersection of Nanbian Rd.
& Buyongsan Rd., Bao'an
Vernacular
1894–1906

江氏大宗祠
宝安区南边路与步涌三路交叉口西南
100米

Ⓧ Line 11
Houting
🚶 后亭站
2.1 km

Located within the Buyong settlement
and the hometown of the Jiang clan, this
courtyard house is one of the very few examples of 'oyster shell houses' remaining
in the Pearl River Delta region. Designed
according to Qing Dynasty architectural
style, the building sits west to east and
covers an area of nearly 460 square metres. The three-door layout is composed
of three halls, arches, four corridors, and
a front patio with a brick and stone arch-
way. Finely decorated, the interiors show
a colourful richness of wooden structures, carvings, glazed tiles, mural paintings, and different materials. Worth the
trip, the gables on both sides are made
of oyster shells mixed with yellow mud,
brown sugar, and steamed glutinous rice.
This material is warm in winter and cool in
summer; it does not accumulate rainwa-
ter, keeping the building dry year round.

**Quanzhi Technology
Innovation Park** »  `111` `G`
Song'an Rd., Shajing St., Bao'an
Mozhao Architects
2016–2018

全至科技创新园
宝安区沙井街道松安路

Ⓧ Line 11
Songgang
🚶 松岗站
1.8 km

Inside one of the many industrial parks in
North Bao'an, the owners improved the
quality of the common facilities by commissioning Mozhao Architects to design
of a couple of buildings that added new
functions to the compound. In the middle of the factory, the former parking lot
was covered with a large landscaped terrace that extends the courtyard space
and increases the spatial quality of the
area, establishing an ample multi-level
public space. Floating walkways connect
the terrace to adjacent buildings, adding
a new layer of accessibility. At the northern border, the architects designed another building that upgrades the program
of the park with a tea house and a show-
room. Composed of six-unit blocks, this
pavilion features plain colours, sloping
roofs, and several inner courtyards, recalling the aesthetic of traditional dwellings in Shajing.

辛桂鹏

All drawings: Mozhao Architects

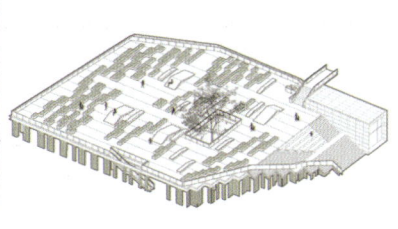

Chao Zhang

Chao Zhang

Extra-SEZ North
Xili, Longhua, Guangming, Guanlan, Buji

H

Birdview of Longhua

Straight from Hong Kong to Beijing via Guangzhou

The northern territories of Shenzhen, separated from the Special Economic Zone by the Tanglangshan Natural Reserve, have undergone a slow but significant development over the twentieth century. It had been slow and unplanned until the pressure of urbanisation came along. With no more free space available inside the SEZ and the intensive urbanisation of Longgang in the north-east and Bao'an in the north-west, the northern-central territory has quickly turned from an agricultural to a high-density productive area of several million inhabitants. This north-central area is physically separated from the SEZ by the inner mountain range, except for two natural plain contact points; one with Luohu and Longgang in the east near Buji town, where the globally famous Dafen Oil Paint Village (see p. 221) is the cradle of the naïf artists' community, as narrated by the movie 'China's Van Goghs' by Yu Haibo and Kiki Tianqi Yu. The other links Nanshan in the west, near Xili town, where the extensive education complex with the Shenzhen Higher Education Mega Centre (see p. 214) and the South University of Science and Technology of China (see p. 216) have been realised

right between two natural reserves. Another pass directly connects the Futian Central District to Longhua near Meilin and is the straight connection between Longhua, Futian, and Hong Kong in the south that makes the area fundamental in terms continental transportation. In the last decade, the new Shenzhen North Station (see p. 213) has become the crossing point for the Hong Kong-Guangzhou-Beijing line, coastal Hangzhou-Fuzhou line, and future Hainan-Shenzhen line. Factories have found a convenient location here; big industrial parks settled their gated compounds in the area, surrounded by a dense urban fabric of housing blocks and 'urban villages'. Nevertheless, despite the roaring urban growth of recent years, the northern mountain crown still hides some natural historical treasures dating back to the early twentieth century republican time. At this time, indigenous villages such as Gangkeng Hakka Town (see p. 212), missionary schools like the Guanpei School (see p. 211), and manufacturing plants like the Guanlan Print Base (see p. 212) were settled halfway between the cities of Guangzhou and Hong Kong, between the Cantonese and British cultures.

112

Dadingling
Shanlin Park

123 County Rd

Jiulong Hill
Golf Club

Longda Expy

SHIYAN

Shenhai Expy

DALANG

Qinh

Fulong Rd

LONGH

Longhua

Longhua Renmin Rd

M

Yangtaishan
Forest Park

Longsheng

Shangtang

LON

Bulo

Xinqu Rd

Hongshan

Xili Golf
Club

118

Changlingpi

122

Xili Lake

Xili Lake

121

120

Tanglang

119

Liuxian Av

Liuxiandong

Xili

Shahe W Rd

University
Town

Fulong Rd

Chuangke Rd

123

XILI

Chaguang

Zhugang

Tanglangshan
Country Park

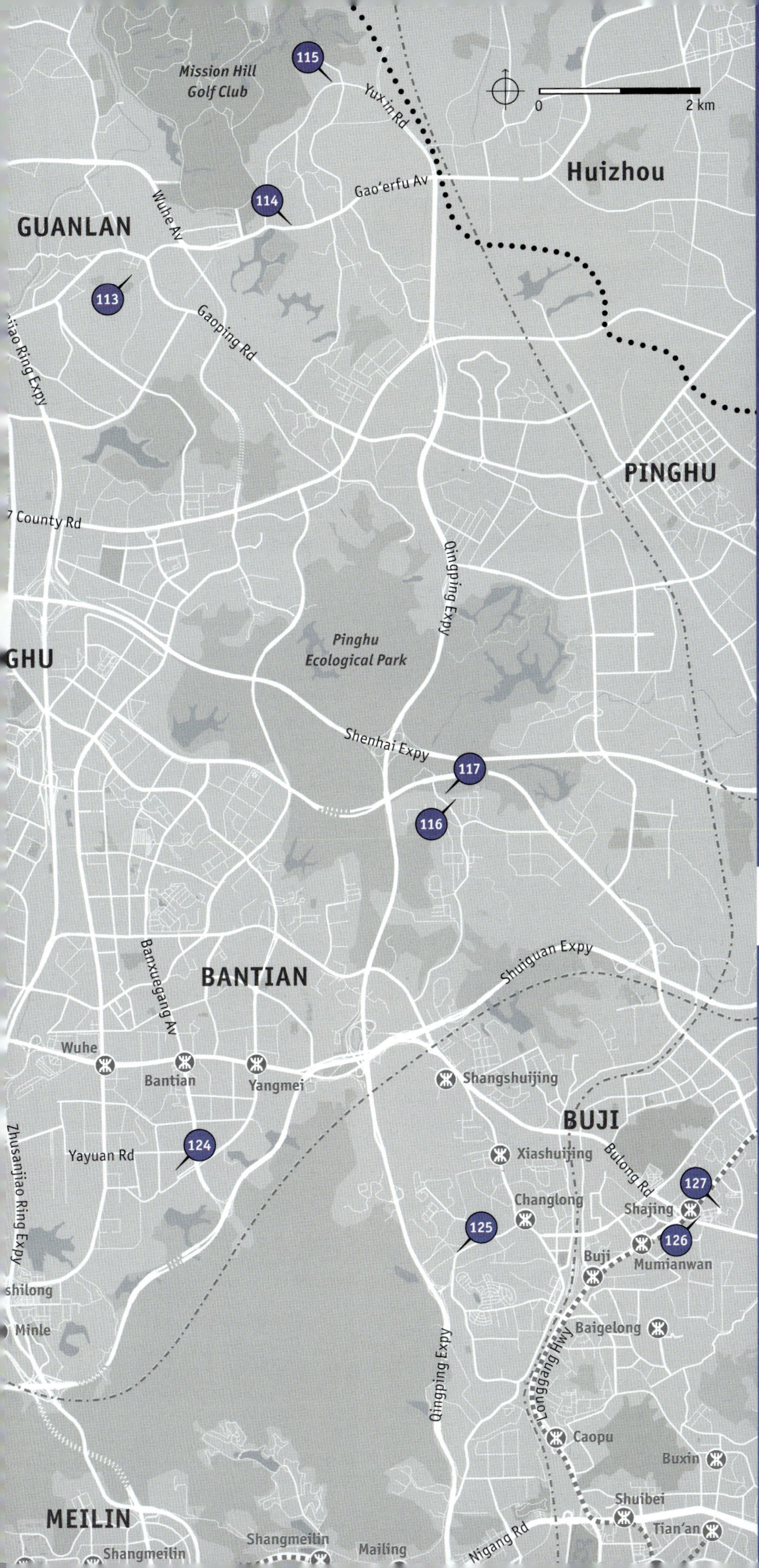

Mission Hill
Golf Club

115

Yux in Rd

Gao'erfu Av

Huizhou

0   2 km

114

Wuhe Av

GUANLAN

113

Gaoping Rd

PINGHU

iao Ring Expy

7 County Rd

Qingping Expy

GHU

Pinghu
Ecological Park

Shenhai Expy

117

116

H

Shuiguan Expy

Banxuegang Av

BANTIAN

Wuhe

Bantian

Yangmei

Shangshuijing

BUJI

Zhusanjiao Ring Expy

Yayuan Rd

124

Xiashuijing

Bulong Rd

shilong

Changlong

Shajing

127

Minle

125

Buji

Mumianwan

126

Baigelong

Qingping Expy

Longgang Hwy

Nigang Rd

Caopu

Buxin

Shuibei

Tian'an

MEILIN

Shangmeilin

Shangmeilin

Mailing

Tower of Spiral

Near No.168, Zhenyuan Rd.,
Guangming

DO Architects
2019

112 H

光明小镇欢乐田园观景台
光明区圳园路168号附近

Line 11
Songgang
松岗站
15.7 km (Bus m490)

In the middle of the Guangming's countryside, at the edge with Dongguan, OCT group invested in the master plan of an Eco-Town in recent years. With high sustainability standards, this development brings together farming, research, residential living, and tourism. The landscape design included a dense pedestrian system encouraging outdoor activities in the countryside where DO Architects designed a sculptural landmark surrounded by crops. Shaped as a 810-degree spiral, the tower is clad with white PTFE film and tensioned metal mesh that hide the inner structural frame and the spiral path that brings visitors up to an observation deck. Although the tower is relatively narrow, the openness of the inner core makes the space dynamic, and one is naturally attracted by the sky above while walking along the ramp with its unusual perspective on the natural landscape.

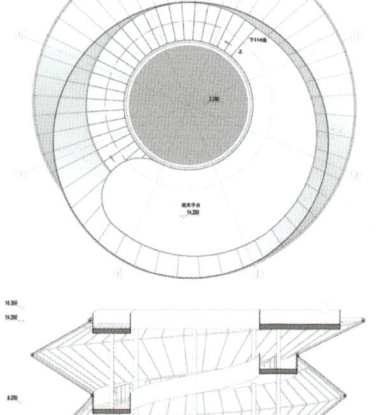

Guanlan Middle School ⩘ ⩘

113 H

1 Yucai Rd., Longhua
Unknown
1930s

市观澜中学
龙华区育才路1号

Line 11
Qinghu
清湖站
13 km (Bus m338)

At the beginning of the twentieth century, a Hakka community settled in northern Longhua district and founded a series of modern educational institutions. Among them, Guanlan Middle School, formerly Zhenneng School, was founded in 1914. Honoured by erudite alumni, it is still running and the historical buildings have been preserved despite recent extension. The main pavilion occupies the barycentric position on the campus; it is a precious heritage of the early republican civic architecture – a long symmetrical building in the compradoric style with a mix of Eastern and Western architectural elements, like arcades and a clock tower.

Guanpei School ⩘

114 H

1 Guangpei N Rd., Guanlan St., Longhua
Niu Hu
1912

广培学校
龙华区观澜街道牛湖社区广培北路

Line 11
Qinghu
清湖站
11 km (Bus m338)

The Guanpei School was built in response to Mr. Sun Yat-sen's slogan 'study to save the country' by Niu Hu, an overseas Chinese erudite. One of the oldest schools in Shenzhen, a 1996 conservation program has brought the school back to its former splendour. The main pavilion has become a symbol and pride of the long-lasting institution. The building recalls the urban architectural style of colonial buildings in Guangzhou and Hong Kong: two storeys high with a double arcade on the main façade, clad in black bricks, sober white plaster moulding, and green balustrade, and a clock tower on top.

H

(Shenzhen Commercial Daily)

(Shenzhen Library)

Guanlan Print Base ☆ | 115 H

Yuxin Rd., Bao'an
Vernacular
1930s

观澜版画村
宝安区裕新路

🚇 Line 11
Qinghu
🚶 清湖站
13 km (Bus m338)

Located in the Longhua countryside, the Guanlan Print Base is the hometown of the famous Hakka printmaker Chen Yanqiao. The cattle village was originally named Dashuitian and is surrounded by water streams and gentle mountains in a perfect *fengshui* environment. The original buildings are still well preserved and feature typical Hakka architectural elements. The site now hosts a cultural museum, print workshops, scenic spots, and other touristic facilities.

Gangkeng Hakka Town ☆ | 116 H

Gankeng Hakka Town, Buji St., Longgang
Vernacular
1700s (2018)

甘坑客家小镇
龙岗区布吉吉华街道甘坑客家小镇内口

🚇 Line 5
Shangshuijing
🚶 上水径站
5 km (Bus 980)

Initially founded by Hakka people from Meizhou, this ancient village is surrounded by a flourishing natural environment with hills, woods, streams, and ditches. In 2016, OCT Group invested 50 million yuan in preserving it and doubling the existing extension to turn it into tourist attraction and cultural spot. This operation partially destroyed its originality, however, several Hakka people still live here and their cultural heritage is kept alive.

Nanxianglou Art Hotel »
117 H

18 Ganli Rd., Gankeng Hakka
Town, Bujijihua St., Longgang
PleasantHouse Design
2018

南香楼艺术酒店
龙岗区布吉吉华街道甘坑客家小镇内甘
李路18号

In the heart of Gangkeng Village, this hotel has taken over Hakka architectural culture, mixing it with contemporary, contrasting elements. Grey tiles, thick wooden doors and beams, and carved details stay together with a pyramid steel-framed glass roofing, creating a recognisable dialogue between old and new. The hotel facilities are organised in a village-like series of buildings linked together by the inner walkways.

Shenzhen North Station ⌄
118 H

Zhiyuan Middle Rd., Longhua
*SUIADR + China Railway 4th
Survey & Design Group*
2008–2013

深圳北站
龙华区致远中路口

 Line 4,5
Shenzhen North
 深圳北站
50 m

Xiao En

The North Station in Longhua District is today the central transportation hub of Shenzhen. Its construction has been part of the planning agenda since the 1990s when the government began working on the 'Beijing-Guangzhou-Shenzhen-Hong Kong Passenger Line'. The station is positioned in the geometric centre of the city, an area that was developed together with the station. The symmetrical composition rules both the architectural and landscape designs and it is coherent with the typical state monumentality of this kind of venue. The station occupies an area of 75,000 square metres; it functions as a multi-layered integration of the railway, bus terminals, metro lines, vehicular circulation, and pedestrian paths. The large square in front of the station welcomes passengers, with terraced gardens and glass elevators connecting the ground level to the ones below. The main building recalls the 'big roof' pavilion shape, while its glazed façade displays the ample concourse with a light, curved steel ceiling.

H

Shenzhen Centre For Design

Shenzhen Higher Education Mega Centre ⋩

?239 Lishui Rd., Nanshan
SZAD + Shenzhen Institute of Building Research
2002–2010

西丽深圳大学城
南山区丽水路2239号（西丽深圳大学城）

🚇 **Line 7**
Xili Lake
🚶 西丽湖站
950 m

Shenzhen has a well-structured set of education facilities. In addition to the central university complex in Nanshan, another cluster is located near Xili Mountain, next to golf courses and a zoo in a natural environment far from downtown. The campus covers an area of nearly 1.5 square kilometres. It is shared by the graduate schools of Peking University, Tsinghua University, Harbin Institute of Technology, and Nankai University. Each institution is an independent campus within the campus, as characterised by the its architectural language. Crossed by a water stream, the central axis and south-east block are the contact points of the three institutions which share resources including the library, the hilly forest, and the sports facilities.

Library of Shenzhen Higher Education Mega Centre »

2239 Lishui Rd., Nanshan
RMJM + SZAD
2007

深圳大学城图书馆
南山区丽水路2239号（西丽深圳大学城）

The 'gateway icon' of the Xili Mega Campus is the library building shared by the four universities on site. It is located in the barycentric point, accessible from all of the different institutions, and acts like a bridge linking them and the other shared facilities together. Its nearly 500-metre-long curved form recalls the topography of the surrounding landscape, while its scale confers a monumental dimension. At the same time, the building's dragon-like shape symbolises the erudite sphere of education and knowledge. Students and faculty use the building as a connective infrastructure across the campus, providing sunshade and protection from the rain depending on the season. The steel structure and concrete structure combine with the glazed façades; the lightness of the matter matches its transparency, creating a sequence of spaces where visitors can experience deep contact with the nature that surrounds them.

Tsinghua University Ocean Centre »

Lishui Rd., Nanshan
OPEN Architecture
2016

121 **H**

清华大学深圳校区海洋大楼
南山区丽水路口

Zhang Chao

H

OPEN Architecture

Next to the library, the Tsinghua Ocean Centre is the deep ocean research base of the Tsinghua Graduate School in Shenzhen. As the last building real-ised on campus, the architects choose to squeeze the built surface on as little land as possible. In doing so, 'the convention-al quad typology for university campus-es is reinterpreted here to form a lively, vertical quad system' where common are-as concentrated in levels are sandwiched between the main research blocks, from the top to the ground. Conference rooms, exhibition spaces, the cafeteria, and oth-er facilities occupy a series of closed and semi-closed areas where greenery en-hances the relaxed atmosphere of the public space. Outside, the exposed con-crete structure declares a sober and long-lasting choice that gently contrasts with the colourful glass of the windows. The brise soleil, which reproduces the rhythm of Debussy's 'Sea' in the angle aperture of each slide, and other shading devices contribute to controlling the building's micro-climate. At the same time, a broad-er set of passive strategies were adopted to lower its energy consumption.

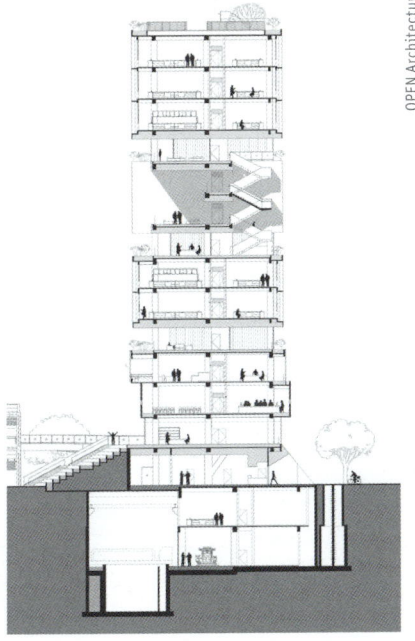

Alex Chan

URBANUS

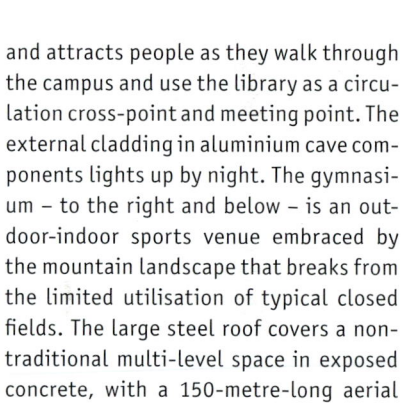

Gymnasium and Library of South University of Science and Technology of China

122 **H**

1088 Xili Xueyuan Ave., Nanshan
URBANUS
2013–2019

南方科技大学体育馆和图书馆
南山区西丽学苑大道1088号（西丽深圳大学城）

Line 5
Tanglang
塘朗站
950 m

Besides the Mega Campus, Xili hosts other universities, such as SUSTech, for which URBANUS designed two of the main campus facilities. Conceived as a porous solid with slightly curved façades, the library (above) condenses together a library, reading areas, an auditorium, a bamboo courtyard, and a series of covered corridors similar to the traditional Cantonese commercial arcades. Such semi-open space suits the rainy sub-tropical weather and attracts people as they walk through the campus and use the library as a circulation cross-point and meeting point. The external cladding in aluminium cave components lights up by night. The gymnasium – to the right and below – is an outdoor-indoor sports venue embraced by the mountain landscape that breaks from the limited utilisation of typical closed fields. The large steel roof covers a non-traditional multi-level space in exposed concrete, with a 150-metre-long aerial looping track that creates a new jogging experience for athletes.

Zeng Tianpei

H

Vanke Cloud City Design Community

Chuangke Rd., Nanshan
UV Architecture + Hua Yi Design + URBANUS (landscape design & master plan)
2019

万科设计公社体育公园
南山区创科路

Line 5
Liuxandong
留仙洞站
1.2 km

Not far from Xili University Town, Vanke has developed a new neighbourhood called 'Cloud City' on a land area that covers nearly 40,000 square metres. As part of this more comprehensive project, UV Architecture designed two plots featuring a complex cluster immersed in an urban park featuring a bus terminal, underground smart parking, private residences, offices, and cultural, commercial, and creative facilities. The main concern behind the design was to achieve sustainable development capable of integrating low-emission goals with high density and environmental qualities. By concentrating the vehicular traffic below ground or under the buildings, the whole cluster is a multi-level pedestrian island. The fragmentation of offices and social spaces creates a town-like rhythm of courtyards. Moreover, the greenery covers roofs and sidewalk paths while a yellow-coloured walking path floats in the sky, connecting the blocks and serving as a strong landmark visible from everywhere.

Zhang Chao

Zhang Chao

H

Zhang Chao

Vanke 5th Park

Hushan Rd., Bantian St.,
Longgang
BIAD + PT Architecture Design
2010–2012

万科第五园景台
龙岗区坂田街道虎山路

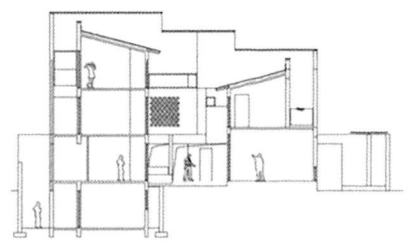

Line 5
Bantian
坂田站
1.5 km

Located north of the Shenzhen SEZ, not far from the North Railway Station, Vanke 5th Park is one of the earliest attempts to put together the instances of real estate and typological research into traditionally dense housing. The critical point of the project was to find a way to design contemporary 'Chinese-style houses' in a market-friendly manner so as to set the path to a coherent local alternative to Western-style conventional designs. In doing so, the designers outlined a vernacular solution that translates six traditional elements of the Chinese built environment into new terms: village, walls, courtyards, neutral colours, climate adaptation, and gardens. Blocks are designed according to a traditional courtyard layout and aggregate in the shape of a village with tiny gardens, narrow streets, and ponds. The aesthetic result is undoubtedly impressive as a poetic meeting of tradition and modernity – despite the evidently poor construction quality.

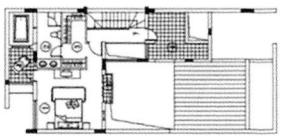

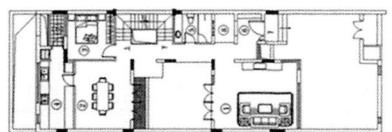

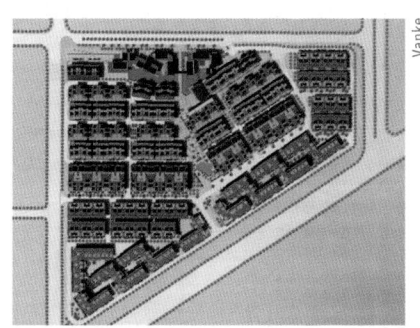

卒佳鹏

Wenbo Palace ⩘

88, Buji W Ring Rd., Longgang
Shenzhen Beauty Group Damao Co.
2017

文博宫
龙岗区布吉西环路88号

 Line 5
Changlong
长龙站
1.1 km

The Wenbo Palace is an antique jewellery and art trading centre designed as a cluster of seven ancient buildings that mix different Chinese dynastic styles. It is an example of architectural *shanzhai* development – a place where you can find merchants, local chess players, and wedding photographers all on the same square. This area mimics an imaginary historical Chinese place.

Dafen Oil Paint Village ⩘

Buji St., Longgang
Informal Village
1990s

大芬油画村
龙岗区布吉街道

 Line 3
Dafen
大芬站
500 m

Most do not know Dafen Village although they may have bought an oil painting replica produced in one of its workshops. Located in Buji Township, Dafen is the mecca of oil painting forgery; its manufacturers export to Asia, Europe, and America, bringing in billions of RMB each year to the area. For this peculiar mix of art, commercialism, and kitsch culture, Dafen is an atypical urban village. Its

H

Wu Qiwei

urban pattern and handshake buildings survived the urban pressure from real estate, and the local community is strong thanks to this shared vocation towards the arts. It does deserve a visit.

Dafen Art Museum
Dafen Oil Painting Village, Buji St., Longgang
URBANUS
2007

127 H

大芬美术馆
龙岗区布吉街道大芬油画村口

On the eastern edge of the village and framed by apartment blocks at its back, the Dafen Art Museum is a sort of artistic temple dedicated to local contemporary art. In its conception, the museum reinterprets the urban and cultural implication of Dafen Village and reckons with the peculiar culture of the place and its reputation, somehow rehabilitating it. Coming from the village, the main façade opens onto a square where community life finds a space to gather and organise public events. From that point, one cannot catch the dimension and complexity of the whole building, a dark-clad, irregular hexagonal solid, which seems to be grafted in the middle of the dense urban

fabric. The program is sandwiched in this cultural and commercial hybrid space that recalls the dual identity of the village. A wide ramp runs around the building and cuts at a top level, connecting the ground floor to the higher backside.

Wu Qiwei

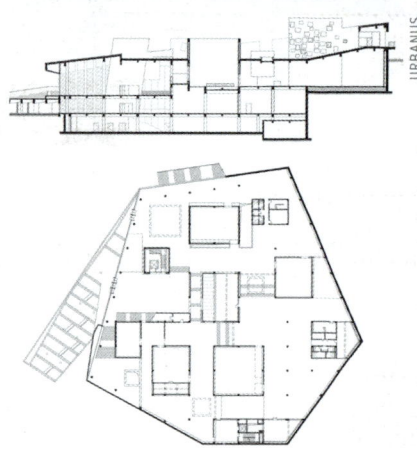

URBANUS

Urban view from subway line 3

I

134 I

Xibu Hakka Dwelling and the Longgang Cultural Centre

The City that Surrounds the Hakka Countryside

Of the many districts in Shenzhen, Longgang and Pingshan most clearly show the consequences of urbanisation's post-reform policies, particularly regarding rural-urban conflicts. Driving from west to east, along the broad avenues connecting the SEZ to the eastern border of the municipal territory like Longgang Avenue or Changshen Expressway, one would see a beautiful mountain landscape surrounding a hilly valley and filled with a clear stratification of built fabrics, including brand-new fancy public venues, recent ordinary housing and office blocks for lease, decades-old factory compounds, mid-2000s handshake buildings, and hundreds of ancient courtyard dwellings nestled between the dense, speculative urban fabrics.

Longgang embodies the duality of being a strongly and quickly urbanised rural area that is now trying to reconquest a cultural identity that looks both beyond and behind. On the one hand, famous architects have been signing landmark projects that will grow the districts' importance, such as the Longgang Cultural Centre (see p. 242) and the Universiade complex which includes the Universiade Village, the Longgang Sports Centre, and the new CUHK campus (see p. 236). On the other side, attempts to preserve the local built heritage have hardly promoted the importance of the rich Hakka architecture that dots the whole valley and its rural ecosystem. Indeed, the local government has struggled to balance real estate development with the conservation of more than one hundred Hakka dwellings in the area. Take the conversion of the Crane Lake Hakka Dwelling (see p. 244) into the Longgang Museum of Hakka Culture, which offers a unique glance of how this area was inhabited before urbanisation.

Suppose the Special Zone is the place of the state and the north-west territory is that of the Cantonese. In that case, northeast Shenzhen is where the Hakka people had flourished and left most traces of their predominancy over east Guangdong Province. Longgang and Pingshan districts mark the last part of the valley's land, connecting the Pearl River to the Mei River basin, nearby the better-known Hakka communities in Fujian and Jiangxi. There are common cultural markers that characterise the Hakka people, such as the language – still popular today among descendants who mostly live abroad – the

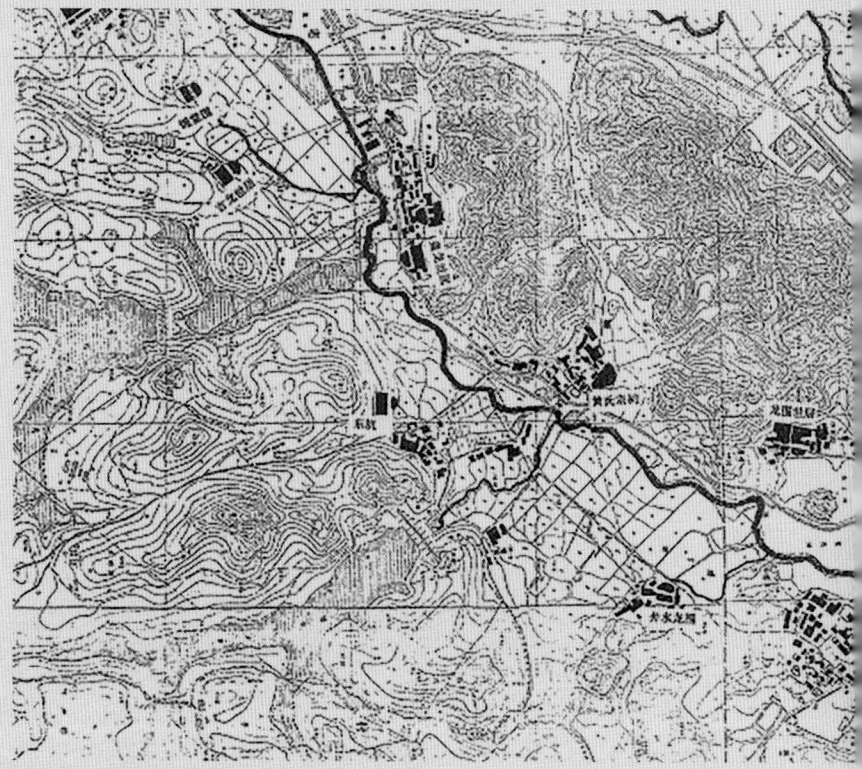

Hakka buildings along Kengzi's Li River Basin

traditional culture, including food, their rural entrepreneurship, and the lineage system that organises society in clans devoted to their ancestors. The Hakka's lineage system constituted the basis of their social and material life. According to this system, the countryside was autonomously managed by a single household whose ancestors had been recognised and appointed by the emperor.

The other peculiar element can be found in Hakka dwellings' architectural typologies, mutated over time and following the place's geographical needs wherever they

settled. In the past, each clan used to live together in a single fortified dwelling. All daily life functions were placed around the ancestor temple in a hierarchical cluster of halls, living units, kitchens, warehouses, courtyards, and animal sheds. In the east Pearl River area, the Hakka developed a system of countryside settlements, made up of clustered fortified villages that were supported by a market town network. An efficient production system allowed the Hakka to flourish in rural trading of products, salt, and artefacts thanks to their wide commercial networks. In this area, Hakka buildings are an evolution from Fujian's famous round *tulou* with a rectangular or semi-circular plan, one to two storeys, and defensive towers at the corners. They follow the cosmological planning principles of *fengshui* by adapting the layout and orientation to the clan's specific needs and the place itself.

The complexity of the plan depends on the dimension and the status of the household and the activities involving the clan. Courtyards act as public outdoors connecting the different areas and, in a symmetrical layout, they all converge at the

Plan of the Crane Lake Hakka Dwelling

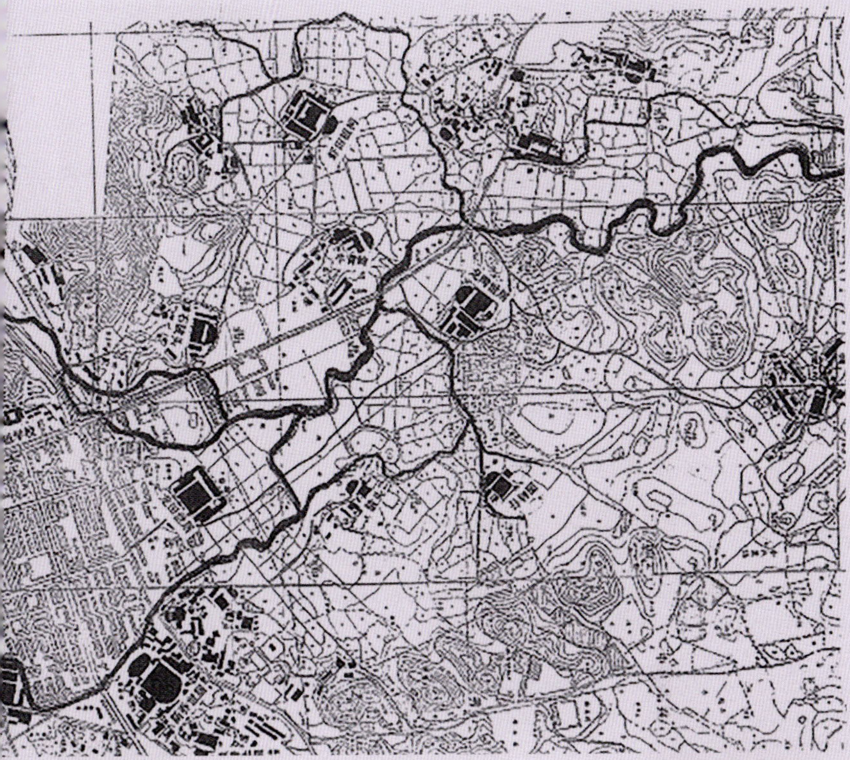

Believed to be in the public domain

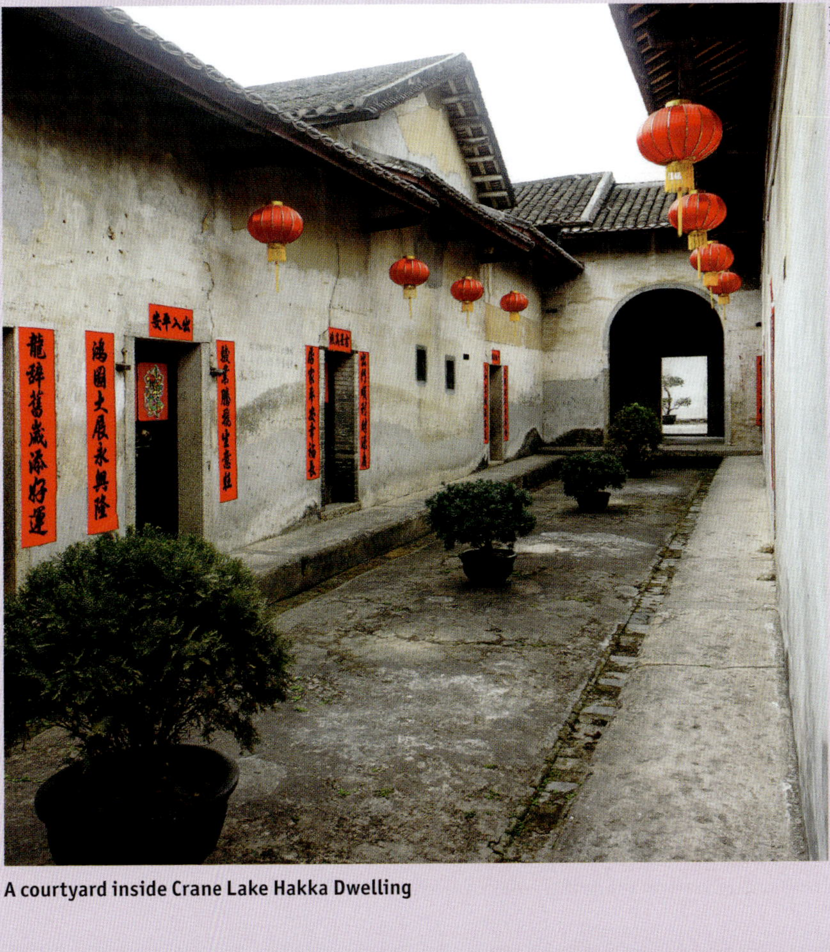

辛佳鹏

A courtyard inside Crane Lake Hakka Dwelling

A courtyard inside Xuanqiang Hakka Dwelling

central hall of the ancestors. Usually, the main façade has one to three gates fronting the *yuechi*, a half-moon pond with an apotropaic value used as a fish reservoir, and the *heiping*, a yard used for public activities and agricultural means. The building's backside is protected by hoods or slopes. The surrounding area used to be rice paddies, orchards, and farms. The construction dates range from 300 to 400 years ago up to modern times, showing various influences and architectural

The Mao's portrait on the wall of a Hakka dwelling in Huiyang

Source: sohu.com

Longtian Hakka Dwelling

evolutions. Defensive structures, indeed, date back to the earliest period of settlement and show more traditional and sober decorative motifs, like calligraphic carved plaques, naturalistic and mythological engravings, and paintings.

Thanks to the fortune of some Hakka entrepreneurs who moved overseas during the colonial time, more recent dwellings show the influx of Western architecture, which results in a mix of eclectically Chinese and foreign architectural elements in unexpected contaminations.

The traditional Hakka life continued until Mao's time when clusters of villages were converted into rural communes.

Although the villages started a slow decay due to occupancy by immigrant peasants from other regions and the exodus of the original households in the newly urbanised areas of the Pearl River Delta, the spatial layout was conserved. Today, if not abandoned, Hakka buildings provide shelter to immigrants who live there in poor conditions. Just a few have been restored or preserved as deserved.

I

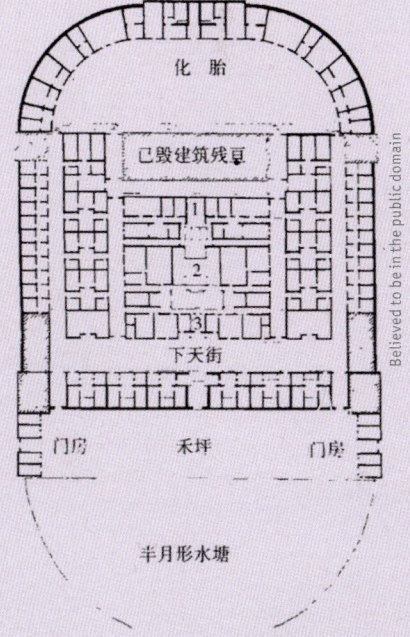

Believed to be in the public domain

Believed to be in the public domain

Plan of Longtian Hakka Dwelling

Plan of Xuanqing Hakka Dwelling

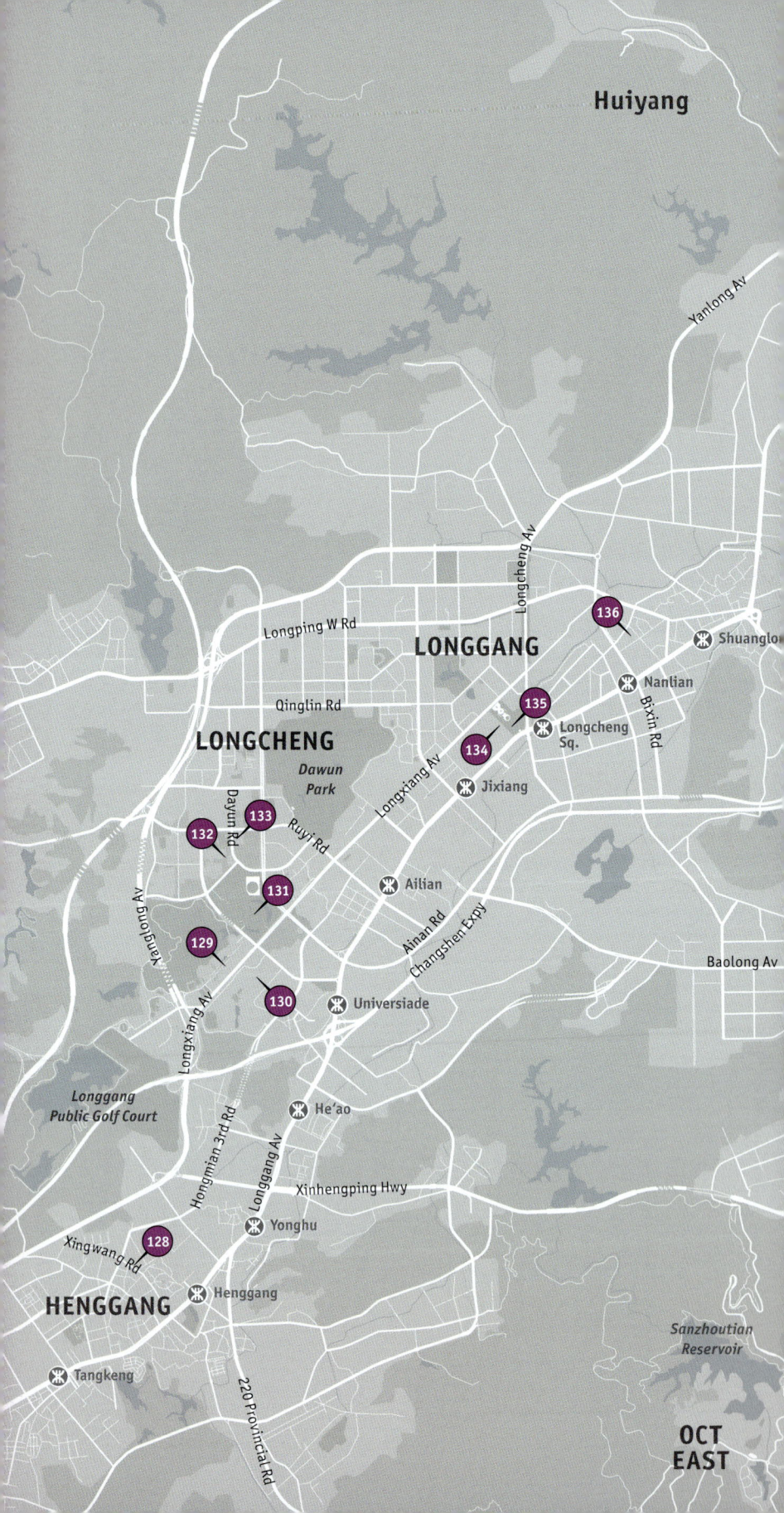

Huiyang

Yanlong Av

Longcheng Av

Longping W Rd

LONGGANG

136

Shuanglo

Nantian

Bixin Rd

Qinglin Rd

135

Longcheng Sq.

LONGCHENG

134

Jixiang

Dawun Park

Longxiang Av

133

132

Dayun Rd

Ruyi Rd

131

Ailian

129

Ainan Rd

Changshen Expy

Baolong Av

130

Yanlong Av

Universiade

Longxiang Av

Longgang Public Golf Court

He'ao

Hongman 3rd Rd

Longgang Av

Xinhengping Hwy

128

Yonghu

Xingwang Rd

Sanzhoutian Reservoir

HENGGANG

Henggang

Tangkeng

220 Provincial Rd

OCT EAST

PINGDI

Shibi Rd

Fuping Rd

138

Huiyang

Huishen Expy

Changshen Expy

141

137

KENZI

6 Country Rd

Guangzu Rd

Danzi Rd

140

139

Lizi Av

Cuijing Rd

Songzikeng
Reservoir

Danzi Rd

Zhanqian Rd

142

Xinhe 4th Rd

Danshui River

Longping Rd

144

Xinhengping Hwy

359 Provincial Rd

I

Jinbi Rd

Jinlong Av

143

Pinglan Rd

PINGSHAN

N.8 Rd

Nanping Expy

Chi'ao
Reservoir

Maluanshan
Countryside Park

MALUAN

0   2 km

Maosheng Hakka Dwelling ⌄ 128 I

Loujiao Third Lane, Longgang
Vernacular
1780

茂盛世居
龙岗区楼角背三巷

Line 3
Henggang
横岗站
1.3 km

Not far from the SEZ, the Maosheng Dwelling is a traditional Hakka house – formerly the home of the He brothers clan – and today serves as a provincial cultural heritage relic. With the typical semi-circular pond at the front and hood at the back, the rectangular enclosure occupies 6,318 square metres at 81 metres wide and 78 long. The perimetral walls are seven metres high, covered by loopholes and with watchtowers at the four corners, showing the strong defence character of the building. Two rings of inner buildings distribute the public and private areas and are used today as living units by immigrants who had already occupied the abandoned building. Despite the alteration that the migrations caused to the building, the original, luxurious decorations still survive in the halls and courtyards. Western-style architectural elements, traditional wood carvings, and coloured details show the He family's past opulence as well as their cultural openness.

Chinese University of Hong Kong – SZ Campus » 129 I

2001 Longxiang Ave., Longgang
Rocco Design Architects Associates with Wang Weijen Architecture + Gravity Partnership
2012–2017

香港中文大学（深圳校区）
市龙岗区龙翔大道2001号

Line 3
Universiade
大运站
1.4 km

Winner of a design competition in 2011, Rocco Design Architects Associates completed this third project of transformation close to the Dayun Natural Park in Longgang. The campus lays at the flat, southern edge of the hill. The different blocks define the edge of the university,

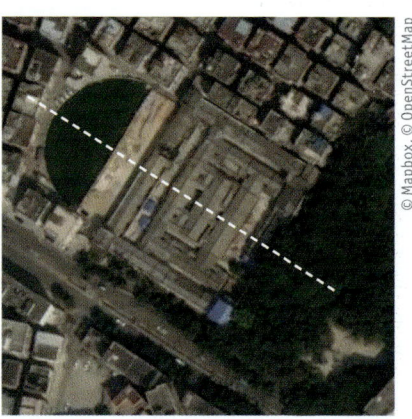

© Mapbox, © OpenStreetMap

辛桂鹏

Chao Zhang

Chao Zhang

creating a strong relationship with the nearby nature and increasing the sense of protection in the college community. The campus is the outcome of a participatory process that involved faculties, students, and clients together with designers. The aim was to identify the different demands and design a sustainable campus with an innovative focus on the community. Following a 'criss-cross' layout, departments, classrooms, and other facilities are located in a flexible, mixed way across the buildings, increasing the interconnection, expansion, and porosity of the design concept. Architect Rocco Yim had previously been working on densification and *mixité*, and, here, he added the natural element to this multi-layered system of spaces and circulation. Hanging walkways and covered bridges link together closed and open spaces in a variety of episodes.

classrooms to students' dorms. A rationalist and sober architecture characterises this quickly built ensemble of blocks surrounded by well-maintained gardens. From the roof deck of the main office block, the tallest building on the campus, it's possible to look onto the nearby CUHK and the iconic Longgang Sports Centre that is just across the street, taking in the mountainous landscape of this part of eastern Shenzhen.

Universiade Village 🛬 130 I

2188 Longxiang Ave., Longgang
CCDI + Shenzhen Construction Design Research + Shenzhen Institute of Building Research
2011

深圳信息职业技术学
龙翔大道2188东门

As part of the 2011 Universiade venues, the Athletes' Village was converted into the Shenzhen Institute of Information Technology at the end of the games. Several buildings compose the campus, each serving a specific function, from teaching

Philipp Meuser

Christian Gahl

Longgang Sports Centre
3001 Longxiang Ave., Longgang
gmp Architekten
2011

大运中心
龙岗区龙翔大道3001

Together with the nearby Universiade Village, the Longgang Sports Centre was completed in 2011 for the occasion of the Shenzhen Universiade. It is located at the eastern end of Dayun Natural Park and physically connects to it through the green corridor covering Longfei Avenue. GMP's design here is both iconic and considerably different from that of Bao'an Stadium (see p. 188), which they designed in Shenzhen in the same year after winning both design competitions. The sports centre consists of a stadium, a swimming pool, a multi-functional hall, and an open-air athletics field. The roof structures of the three main buildings are designed as steel prismatic shells with triangular glass facets. The sculptural shapes are emphasised by illumination at night, which makes them shine as white diamonds in the darkness. The main stadium has a total capacity of 60,000 people and a diameter of 310 metres on the longest side. Inside, the prismatic structure is exposed, and the perception at night is that of translucent, luminous ceilings cantilevered on the sports field. Surrounded by the mountainous landscape, artificial lakes and ponds are linked to the stadia by greenery, suggesting a formal dialogue with the environment, in a balance between anthropic and natural.

gmp Architekten

Christian Gahl

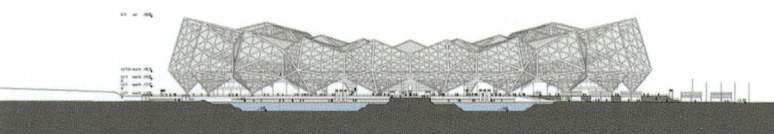

gmp Architekten

Philipp Meuser

Maluanshan

132 Exhibition Centre of Shimao Shenzhen-Hong Kong International Cen

131 Longgang Sports Centre

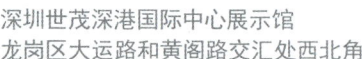

Exhibition Centre of Shimao Shenzhen-Hong Kong International Centre

132 I

Intersection of Dayun Rd. & Huangge Rd., Longgang
SHUISHI
2019

深圳世茂深港国际中心展示馆
龙岗区大运路和黄阁路交汇处西北角

 Line 3
Universiade
大运站
3 km

Between the Longgang Sports Centre and the Shenzhen Sports School, this building is the public hub of Shimao Group. It is designed to attract attention by day and night, thanks to its fragmented shape and transforming façades. Combining tradition and technology on one side, the architects translated the traditional culture of 'spiral scrolls and layered gardens' by designing multiple terraced roofs looking onto the landscape. On the other side, they adopted a double-curtain wall system with LED transparent screens to form a hazy paper canvas that displays digital dynamic images simultaneously inside and outside the building and lights up once night falls.

Lin Lv

130 Universiade Village

129 Chinese University of Hong Kong

Lin Lv

The Coli Pavilion Hotel »

168 Dayun Rd., Longgang
China Overseas Real Estate Group
2011

133 I

中海聖廷苑酒店
龙岗区大运路168号

 Line 3
Universiade
 大运站
4 km

Behind the Longgang Sports Centre, the Coli Pavilion Hotel stands decontextualised as a minaret in the desert. Far from showing any contemporary aesthetics, the building exterior interprets the Deco style of the 1930s, although the media presents it as a Spanish-style hotel. On the four-storey square basement stands a 26-storey rectangular tower block containing 400 rooms.

Philipp Meuser

I

Longgang Cultural Centre

134 I

8028 Longxiang Ave., Longgang
Mecanoo
2019

龙岗区公共艺术与城市规划馆
龙岗区龙翔大道8028号

Line 3
Longcheng Sq.
龙城广场站
700 m

Located on a narrow site with strict height restrictions, the Longgang Cultural Centre connects the different urban fabrics of the district and contributes greatly to the community's cultural life. The long, sinuous shape of the building is an iconic landmark, and the red colour of the cladding stands out from the greyness of the surroundings. Its curved edges and tilting façades generate new frames on the urban landscape, mitigate the climate,

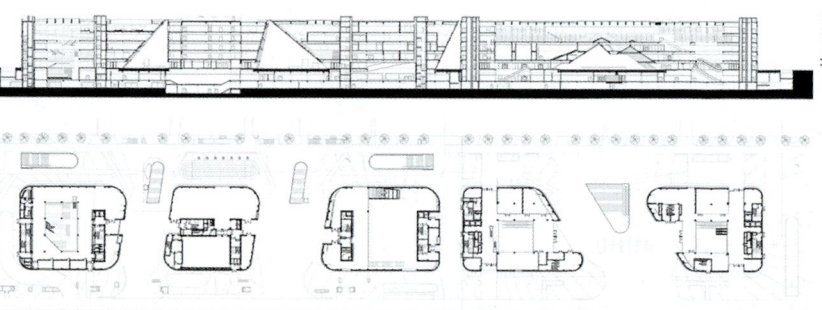

and guide the pedestrian connections across the public space at the two sides of the building. As the four blocks suggest, the centre combines four significant functions: a museum, a young centre, a science hub, and a book mall. The entrances are located at the sheltered squares, where activities can extend to the outdoors. The *in situ* concrete structure shows all of its beauty inside. It is intentionally designed to evoke visitors' emotions, thanks to the sculptural shape. At the top of each building, the tilted full-height interior spaces host galleries and exhibition halls where the structural aesthetic is especially enjoyable.

element directing pedestrians from the square to the commercial gallery, especially by night when the artificial lighting is on. The square layout contrasts with the innovative architectural solution for the mall. It organises the space symmetrically along a 45-degree southeast axis. It shows the post-modernist taste of past decade's urban design while quoting the cosmological scheme of ancient ritual and imperial compounds. Two fountains lay along this axis, acting as focal centres of the orthogonal-grid gardens and decorated with colonnades and zoomorphic sculptures.

Longcheng Plaza

135 I

120 Qianxiang Rd., Longgang
Ingame
2017

龙城广场
市龙岗区向前路120号

At the eastern side of the Longgang Cultural Centre, the Longcheng Plaza creates a square-like public space between the cultural venue and the new skyscrapers on Dezheng Road. Developed by Vanke, what looks like an ending terrace on the square is actually the roof garden of a semi-outdoor shopping mall that, in its open-air section, is covered by a cluster of hexagonal umbrellas. These shelter the atrium space from rain, direct sunlight, and create a visible architectural

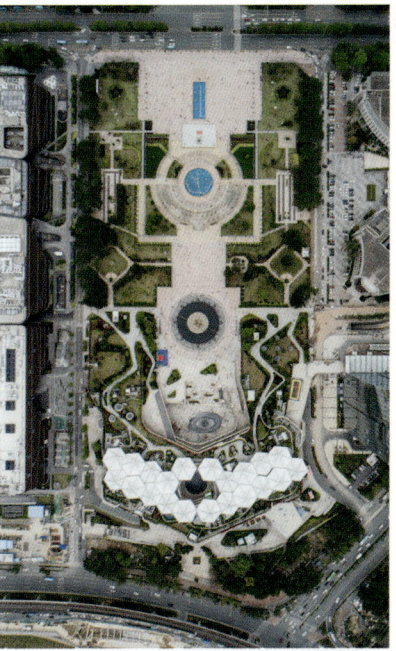

BaiYu

I

BaiYu

Crane Lake Hakka Dwelling (Longgang Museum of Hakka Culture)

136 I

1 Luoruihe N St., Nanlian Community, Longgang
Vernacular
1817

龙岗客家民俗博物馆
龙岗区南联社区罗瑞合北街1号

Line 3
Nanlian
南联站
1 km

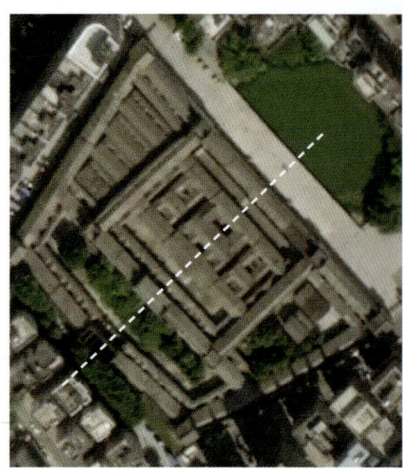

The Crane Lake residence is the largest Hakka dwelling in the country in addition to being the most extensive ethnographic museum dedicated to Hakka culture. At 166 metres wide by 109 metres long, it is an outstanding example of a castle-style Hakka enclosure. Its external wall resembles a silver ingot shape: wide in the front and narrow at the back, with four watchtowers at the corners. Inside, the inner walls frame a rectangular sequence of courtyards, corridors, rooms, and wells in various sizes, staggered like in a maze. With an area of nearly 25,000 square metres, the building was constructed in 10 years by the Luo clan. It was intended to house nearly 200 family members inside its 300 rooms. According to its hierarchical and functional layout, the side wings are home to production and defence, while the middle and back areas are for private lodging, and, finally, the core area for ritualistic and formal activities. Today, the dwelling is embedded in the dense Longgang District. Fronted by its traditional water pond, it is very well preserved. Since its transformation into a museum in 1992, several rooms have become exhibition halls where more than 400 original Hakka relics are on display. The restoration has maintained the sobriety of the architectural style, intensified by the presence of furniture, labour tools, handicrafts, and art pieces.

144 I

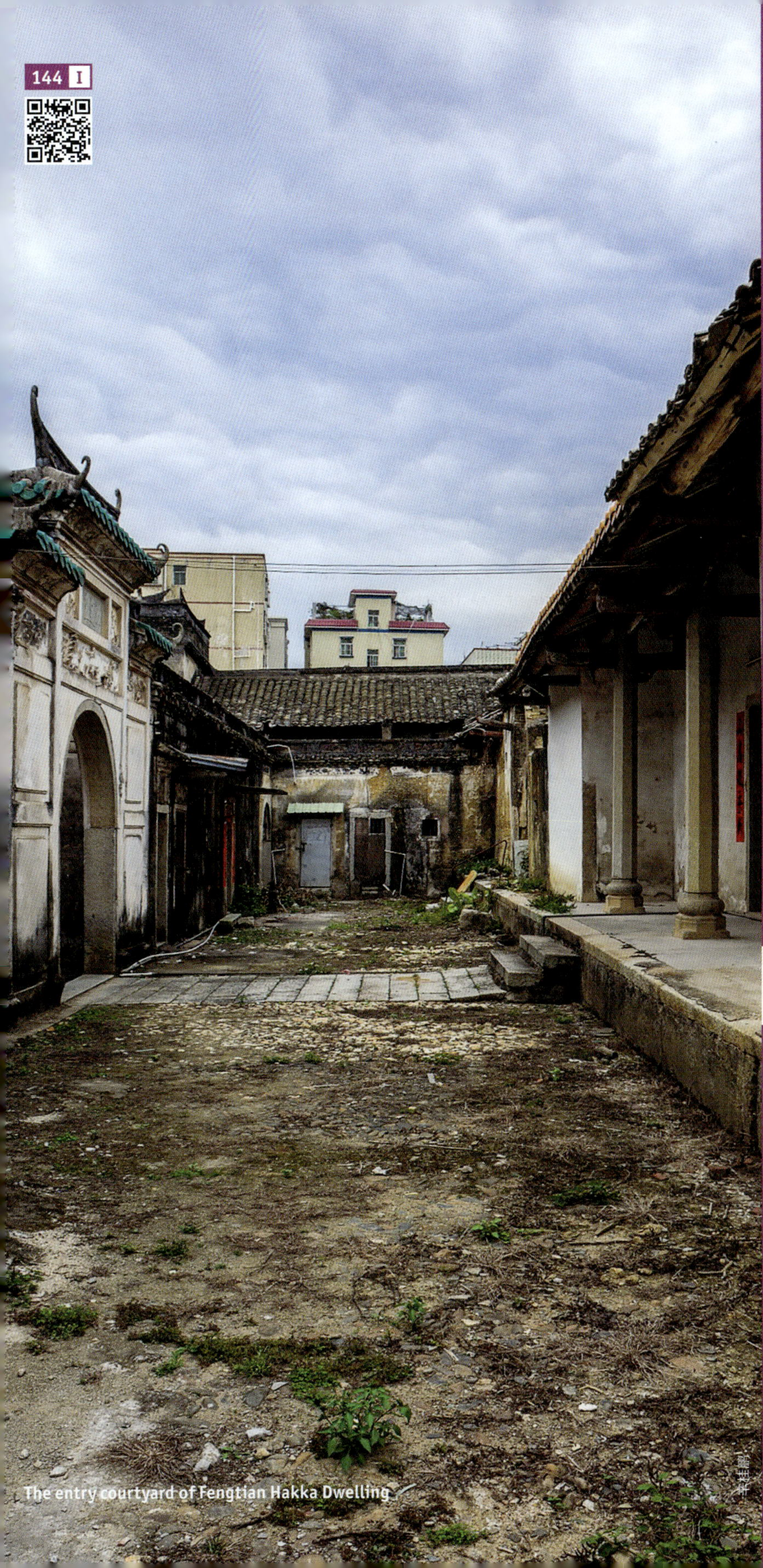

The entry courtyard of Fengtian Hakka Dwelling

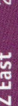

Xuanqing Hakka Dwelling ⌄

East Lane, Shabeiyu, Longgang
Vernacular
1936

璇庆新居
龙岗区沙背坜东巷

Line 3
Shuanglong
双龙站
3.5 km (Bus m305)

This small dwelling has one of the most singular decorative apparatuses visible in Shenzhen, although, in recent years, it has been incorrectly used as a workshop. Built by a Sino-Malaysian Hakka merchant in the 1930s, the building shows a stylistic blend of Chinese, Arab, and Western elements that must have made it exotic and wealthy. Although the water pond in the front was filled and replaced with a factory building, the external walls still show two watchtowers at the corners that are four storeys high with three levels of gun holes. On the main façade, the main gate is framed by a Western pronaos with Arabesque arches and Chinese Baroque gables with bas-relief floral patterns. Covered by a blue-tiled roof, the building is a reinforced concrete structure – quite unusual for the time and context.

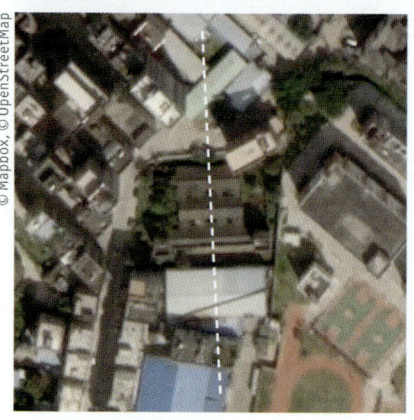

Jikeng Hakka Dwelling ⌄

Jikeng Rd., Longgang
Vernacular
1824

吉坑世居
龙岗区吉坑路

Line 3
Shuanglong
双龙站
9.5 km (Bus m279)

The Jikeng Dwelling is a castle-style Hakka enclosure built by the Xiao family from Ning, Fujian. The building is not well preserved, but it is entirely unaltered. At 45 degrees west to south and foregoing the typical pond and yard, the structure is 67 metres wide and 72 metres long. Its outer wall has a single gate on the main façade and two more gates on the sides that are concealed behind the two corner turrets. The three main halls divide the inner space and organise the hierarchy of functions. The back hall – a shrine to deities and ancestors – and towers are three storeys high, standing out from the other two-storey blocks. The boat-shaped ridge marks the fragmented roofs and engravings, such as wealth and longevity, decorate the doors and archways, evoking poetry from the delicate, sober apparatus.

辛桂鹏

Shenzhen Centre For Design

© Mapbox, © OpenStreetMap

© Mapbox, © OpenStreetMap

China Resources Archives Library

139 I

Daya Bay, Huiyang District, Huizhou
Studio Link-Arc
2018

华润大学图书馆
惠州市惠阳区大亚湾华润大学

Line 3
Shuanglong
双龙站
49 km (Bus e33+268)

Shengliang Su

Shengliang Su

Fifty kilometres east of Longgang District, in Huizhou municipality, there is a significant chemical industry facing Daya Bay. There, the China Resources University was recently founded, commissioning its architectural development to famous architects like the London-based firm Foster + Partner, who designed the general master plan of the campus, and Studio Link-Arc. The campus sits on a terraced site with dramatic views of the sea. While Foster designed a horizontal cluster of rationalist buildings in clay bricks, Studio Link-Arc designed the 9,000-square-metre archive as a multilevel building climbing up the hillside, with a plastic composition of blocks clad in homemade grey bricks. The interior reflects the volumetric modelling of the exterior. It shapes the program's variety at different levels which are all connected by the spectacular vertical golden volume of the main staircase.

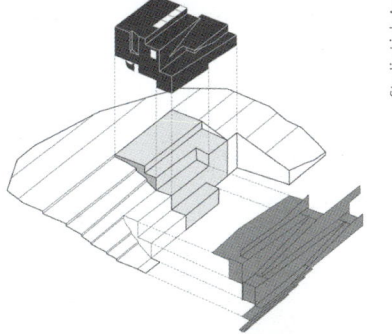

Studio Link-Arc

I

Shengliang Su

豐田世澤

豐田世澤　　　五夏家聲

辛佳鵬

© Mapbox, © OpenStreetMap

© Mapbox, © OpenStreetMap

Rongtian Hakka Dwelling «≫ 140 I

Tianduanxin Village, Longtian
St., Pingshan
Vernacular
1908

荣田世居
坪山区龙田街道田段心村

Line 3
Shuanglong
双龙站
15.5 km (Bus e21/366)

Longtian Hakka Dwelling ≫ 141 I

Tianduanxin Village, Longtian
St., Pingshan
Vernacular
1837

龙田世居
坪山区龙田街道田段心

Line 3
Shuanglong
双龙站
13.5 km (Bus e21/366)

I

Positioned at 35 degrees north-east to south-west, the Rongtian Dwelling takes its name from the reddish colour of its main façade. At 73 metres wide by 80 metres deep, it has a castle-style shape that is low in the front and high in the back, facing the typical water pond. Three stone-framed arched gates on the main front give access to the first courtyard, connected to the inner enclosure of the Huang's ancestral hall. The decorative apparatus is conserved with finely engraved wooden frames, colourfully painted eaves, carved beams, and boat-shaped ridge roofs in grey tiles. During the Great Leap Forward in 1962, the building was transformed into a rural commune; some traces are visible on the pink walls today.

One of the most well-preserved enclosures in Shenzhen, the Longtian Dwelling is a castle-style enclosure with peculiar characteristics. At 66 metres wide and 73 deep, it consists of three main halls, four transversal wings, an outer perimetral ring, four corner towers, two small external enclosures, mooring rivers, and dykes all around. Under protection since 1987, the watercourse's rural character marked the limits of urbanisation. The main façade anticipates the building's magnificence: three arched gates, boat-shaped ridge roofs, engravings, and watchtowers topped with pot-ear side walls. Despite partially collapsed structures, the architectural elements are still visible inside all rooms and courtyards.

Pingshan Library ⌄
Huide Rd., Pingshan, Longgang
URBANUS
2015–2018

142 I

坪山图书馆
坪山区汇德路

Line 3
Shuanglong
双龙站
8.5 km (Bus m497)

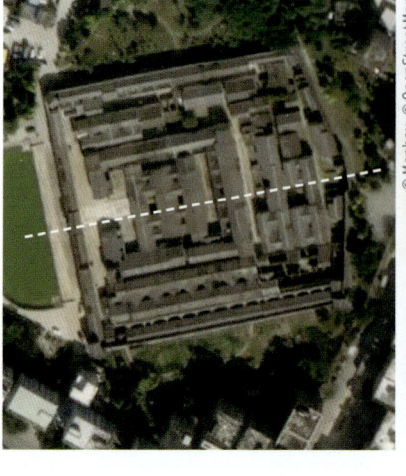

The Pingshan Library is next to the Pingshan Performing Arts Centre by OPEN Architecture and the Pingshan Art Museum by Vector Architects, together known as Pingshan Cultural Complex, located directly in front of the Grand Industrial Zone Central Park. The district's industrial vocation has attracted young people here, and this cultural cluster represents the 'acropolis of this highland'. Designed as a 'sponge-like porous space', the wall-like set of buildings creates an open walk-through space where citizens can wander all day long. The museum, the library, a conference centre, and community halls are found inside three compact buildings that organise such functions vertically. Each block has its own aesthetical identity and orientation, although they all contribute to the continuity in architectural language. The open space connecting all of the buildings creates a village-like layout, echoing the local cultural tradition of the Hakka settlements.

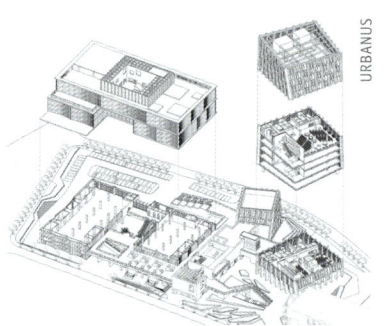

Dawan Hakka Dwelling ⌂☆» 143 Ⅰ

Dawan Rd., Longgang
Vernacular
1791

大万世居
坪山区马大万路

🚇 Line 3
Shuanglong
双龙站
🚶 9.4 km (Bus e21+b952)

With 400 rooms and a covered area of 25,000 square metres, this castle-style Hakka building is one of the most important and well-preserved in Shenzhen. Built by the Zeng family, it features three gates, four gun towers, the typical half-moon pond, and an ancestral hall. It retains historical relics and allows for the study of folk costumes and Hakka culture.

Fengtian Hakka Dwelling « 144 Ⅰ

Fengtian Village, Pingshan
Vernacular
1799

Ⅰ

丰田世居
坪山区丰田世居

🚇 Line 3
Shuanglong
双龙站
🚶 8.5 km (Bus m277)

The Fengtian Dwelling was built by the Huang clan and, at its greatest splendour, nearly 700 family members inhabited this castle-style enclosure. Today, the exteriors display the original richness of the building while the interiors have mostly collapsed. Despite the poor conservation, the building is surrounded by a notable landscape with Pi Mountain behind it and a half-moon pond at the front facing the open urban space – a reminder of the site's original *fengshui* structure.

The *heiping* in front of Fengtian Hakka Dwelling

I

辛桂鹏

J

A panoramic road in Dapeng

The Yellow Sea Coast

Far from the noisy and stressful life of downtown and the industrial northern areas of the city, Shenzhen's eastern coast is a hidden treasure – full of naturalistic and architectural jewels. Spread along more than 150 kilometres of coastline, the natural morphology of the territory is at the base of the physical isolation of Yantian and Dapeng from the rest of the city.

The mountains contain the narrow strip of land facing the sea, in a multitude of sinuous coves and natural harbours. The mountain slope sinks below the sea hiding, cove after cove, the presence of ancient and modern settlements, including the Mirs Bay Overseas Chinese Cemetery (see p. 264) and the mid-twentieth-century Honghua Dyeing Factory, today known as iD Town (see p. 266). To the west, Shatoujiao Port had been one of the oldest checkpoints with Hong Kong, becoming a cultural bridge between the British colony and Cantonese community and allowing the transit of people and goods even before the birth of Shenzhen. Yantian Port, indeed, is the major port of the city today as it manages the freight traffic on the South China Sea and

the far-east routes. To the east, Dapeng Peninsula reaches Huiyang, a district of Huizhou, which is today the core of the largest local Hakka community. The mountains gave protection to the inland countryside settlements, while the coast served as a door to marine trade and an outpost against the Japanese pirates who would raid the South China Sea. Dapeng Fortress (see p. 269) is the best example of the defensive presence along the coast, dotted by several historical buildings that served for that purpose, like the headquarters of the Dongjiang Column, a division of the Anti-Japanese Aggression Guerrilla Force, set up in 1939 near the now Art Inn Guesthouse (see p. 265).

The natural beauty of the place has made it Shenzheners' top weekend-escape destination. Hawaiian-like beaches feature Western-style vacation atmospheres and are a good starting point for discovering the area. Indeed, Dameisha, the main beach, condensed into just two square kilometres plenty of hotels, an outlet village, fancy apartments, and, surprisingly, the Vanke Centre (see p. 260), which is the company's headquarters from which lucky employees overlook the sea all day.

J

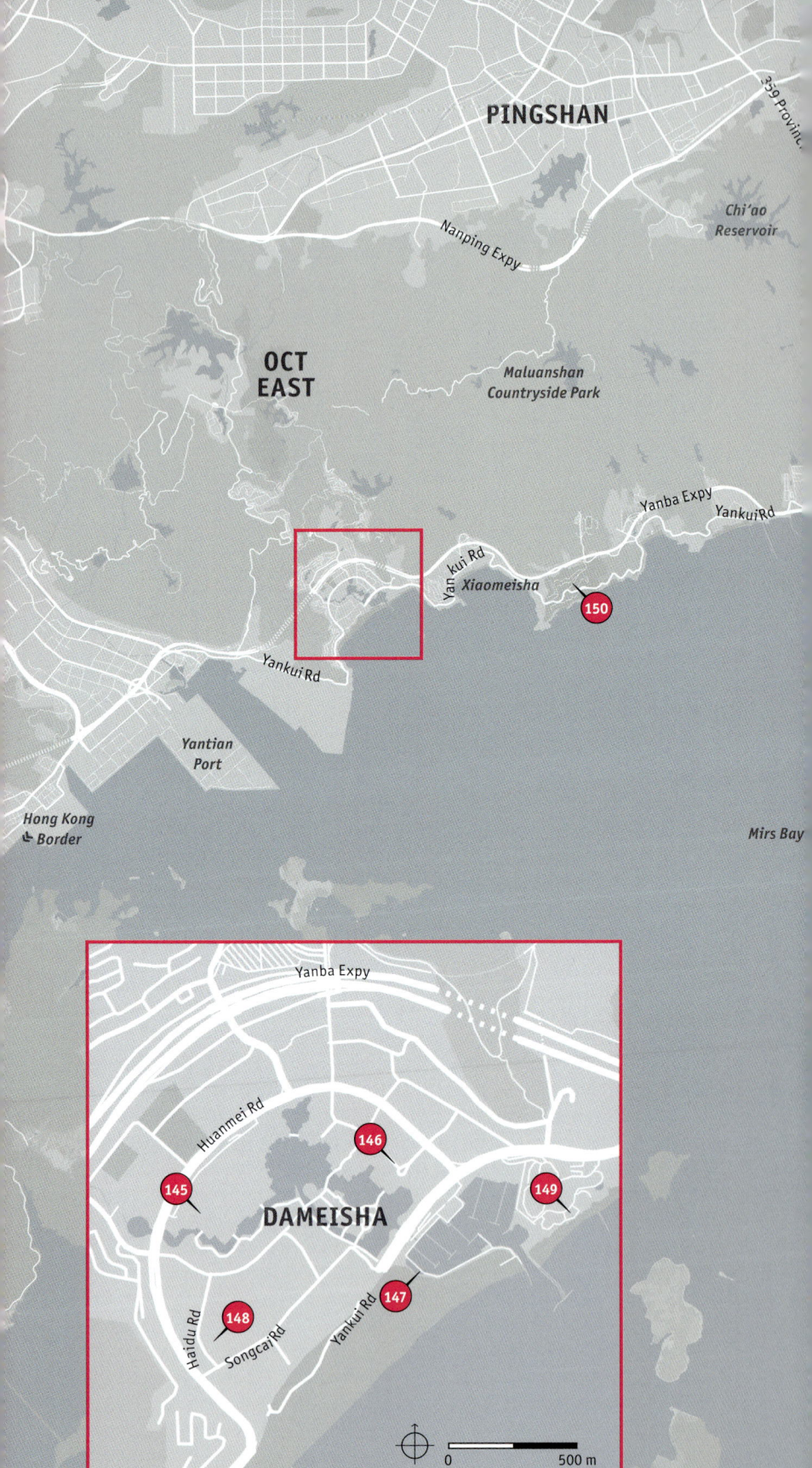

PINGSHAN

359 Provin...

Chi'ao
Reservoir

Nanping Expy

OCT
EAST

Maluanshan
Countryside Park

Yanba Expy

YankuiRd

Yan kui Rd

Xiaomeisha

150

Yankui Rd

Yantian
Port

Hong Kong
↳ Border

Mirs Bay

Yanba Expy

Huanmei Rd

146

145

DAMEISHA

149

Haidu Rd

148

Songcai Rd

Yankui Rd

147

0   500 m

Huiyang
(Huizhou)

SHAOGUI

Daya
Bay

JICHONG

Kuiba Tunnel

Yanba Expy

TUYANG

151

Kuipeng Rd

DAPENG
FORTRESS

154

Pengfei Rd

153

152

Die fu Rd

DAPENG

359 Provincial Rd

Daya
Bay

156

Nan'ao Xindong Rd

155

Dapeng Peninsula

J

359 Provincial Rd

DONGCHONG

South China
Sea

0   2 km

Vanke Centre

Huanbi Rd., Dameisha, Yantian
Steven Holl
2006–2009

145 J

万科东海岸
盐田区大梅沙环碧路口

Line 8
Dameisha
大梅沙站
1.3 km

Completed in the same year as the Linked Hybrid in Beijing, the Vanke Centre is the first building by American architect Steven Holl in China. With a scale factor that dominates Dameisha beach, this building was conceived as a 'horizontal skyscraper – "as long as the Empire State Building is tall"'. Lying between the mountains and the seashore, its flat profile dialogues with nature; it seems as if it once floated on a higher sea. Sloping gardens and ponds design the outdoor offering much space to the public below, above, and around the building. The whole structure is cantilevered off a few giant pillars that condense all vertical circulation between the floating blocks, the ground, and the underground facilities. The fragmentation into irregular blocks amplifies the dramatic shape of this architecture. Thanks to such dynamism, the perception of the surrounding landscape is never the same. Moreover, it reveals the sophisticated functional

program that comprises the hotels, spas, apartments, and Vanke headquarters. The centre is an excellent example of technological innovations that create a dynamic interaction between architectural elements and climatic conditions. Structurally speaking, it is a combination of cable-stay bridge technology merged with a high-strength concrete frame. The first building in southern China to be rated LEED platinum, it is a tsunami-proof hovering building. It features an integrated system of sustainable devices that improve energy and water efficiency, reduce the heat island effect, and control the indoor environmental quality. Inside, every detail is by design, from the door handlings to the local bamboo furniture.

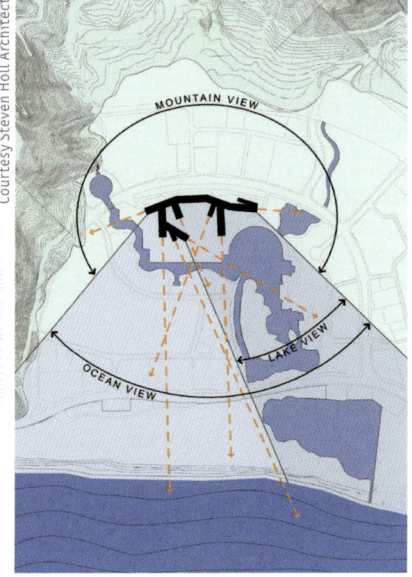

J

Philipp Meuser

80 Step Apartments by the Sea «

146 J

Dameisha S Inner Ring Rd.,
Yantian
OCT
2009–2011

八十步海寓
大梅沙内环路南

Walking from the Vanke Centre to the beach, a public park with an artificial lake connects Steven Holl's building to a scenery that resembles a Mediterranean village. Low apartment blocks with commercial basements frame curvy pedestrian paths articulated with bridges, micro-squares, pergolas, bell towers, fountains, and other scenic spots. The architectural and landscape designs mimic an imaginary, faraway place, where locals live and spend time. At the same time, the designs replicate the cliché, exotic scenographies of many other residential communities spread around the city. Nevertheless, the integration within the context makes you genuinely feel somewhere else, producing a sense of displacement and curiosity.

Dameisha Wishing Tower «

147 J

9 Yanmei Rd., Dameisha, Yantian
Gensler + SZAD
1999

大梅沙愿望塔
盐田区大梅沙盐梅路9号口

Dameisha is a beach area – similar to the ones in Western countries, though unique to Shenzhen – where people come to enjoy the holiday atmosphere of an exotic marine paradise. Here, along the promenade framing the sandy beach, the Wishing Tower spires towards the sky. Its open steel frame is 81 metres high and supports the vertical connection to a three-lever observation glass box that dominates the small bay. With a shape echoing that of a torch, the tower is a focal landmark for the whole area.

CreatAR Images

His House and Her House

148 J

79 Dameisha Village, Yantian
Wutopia Lab
2017

欲望之屋
盐田区大梅沙村79号口

Walking inside Dameisha Village, mainly built in the 1990s, a couple of coloured buildings stand out from the others' pale cladding. These two buildings painted in blue and pink are the outcome of a regeneration attempt that was promoted for the occasion of the 2017 Shenzhen Biennale. The village indeed is struggling to maintain its consistency under the pressure of the real estate market that would destroy the informal settlement in order to make space for fancy developments. The architects created a new identity for the buildings by using the two colours that commonly symbolise masculine and feminine. In doing so, they visually narrate two different ways to process food in the local culture, which was the topic of the Biennale: public kitchens where men used to prepare durable food like bacon and beer, and private kitchens where women used to cook meals for the family. The small, open space between the two buildings is a square where locals come together, socialise, and recognise themselves as a community.

J

CreatAR Images

Sheraton Dameisha ⌄
9 Yankui Rd., Dameisha, Yantian
Farrells
2007

149 J

梅沙京基喜来登度假酒店
盐田区盐葵路大梅沙段9号

Right on the beach and not far from the Wishing Tower, this 12-storey hotel is the largest in Dameisha. Its curvaceous form does not just maximise the sea view onto Mirs Bay, but it also creates a gentle relationship with the natural setting, making waves the central architectural theme inside and outside of the building. With an all-glass façade on both sides, the curved block lodges all rooms. It stands on a massive stone-clad basement, home to five-star facilities and surrounded by exotic landscaping.

Mirs Bay Overseas Chinese Cemetery ⌃
Yankui Rd., Yantian
OCT
2005

150 J

大鹏湾华侨墓园
盐田区盐葵路

Line 8
Xiaomeisha
小梅沙站
3 km

Driving along the coast from Dameisha to Dapeng, cove after cove, the Mirs Bay Cemetery lies on the mountain slope that sinks below the sea. Built by the real estate company, OCT, as a privileged cemetery, it features all the traditional characteristics of Chinese burial typology combined with the typical extensiveness

Philipp Meuser

and density of Western cemeteries. The layout follows the natural semi-circular shape of the small bay. Several levels create a terraced amphitheatre facing the sea and backed by Meishajian Mountain, according to the best *fengshui*.

Art Inn Guesthouse 151 J

20 Huyuan Rd., Guanhu Village, Dapeng
Aether Architects
2017

深圳艺栈ARTINN民宿
大鹏区葵涌街道官湖村湖园路20号

Line 8
Tuyang
土洋沙站
6 km

Formerly an abandoned fishermen's village, this diffused hostel accommodates its functions in the old houses, recreating a sense of continuity inside the town. The architects wisely applied the principle of originality, keeping the existing structure as it is and grafting new elements, with no ambiguity between them. What attracts the most attention is the raw truss structures painted in white that wrap one of the buildings, thereby creating new architectural spaces in between the public and private ones. Rooms, a café, an art gallery, and an open-air theatre are all spread around the area, while kept together by a continuous visual connection generated by the metal structures running along the roof tops and the balconies on the ground.

J

iD Town (Mingde Academy)

106 Kuipeng Rd., Longgang
O-office Architects
2014–2019

iD TOWN 国际艺术区
龙岗区葵鹏路No.106号

Line 8
Tuyang
土洋沙站
4.5 km

Located near the Dapen Peninsula, inside an almost-pristine wooded valley, the so-called iD Town originally was the site of the former Honghua Dyeing Factory. Here, immigrant labourers used to work during the early industrialisation of Shenzhen. Then, after several years of abandonment, the Guangzhou-based firm O-office was called to design the renovation and reactivation of this eight-hectare area. The site itself shows a unique architectural aesthetic as an industrial relic, and the architects reinforced this character by restructuring the spatial narrative and declaring the contrast between old and new materiality. What we see now is the Mingde Academy – the completion of a two-phase process that allowed the slow refurbishment of the site, with different alternating functions chosen according to the selected programs. At the beginning, the architects cleaned up the site and transformed two buildings: the main dyeing building was turned into a creative compound with an art gallery and several workshops, and the former workers' dormitory became a youth hostel; today it is the student dorm. Later, they completed the renovation of the remaining buildings to host the current educational institution. As an experimental school, teaching buildings, dormitories, and facilities are organised inside the former factory pavilions surrounded by the natural forest and connected through it. A 'forest promenade' sporadically connects all buildings and outdoor facilities, with an alternation of hanging walkways, stairs, and ramps that influence perceptions of nature in unconventional and imaginative ways. Raw materials, acid colours, and lucid and opaque effects all contribute to strengthening the dialogue between new and old.

Zhang Chao

Wu Siming

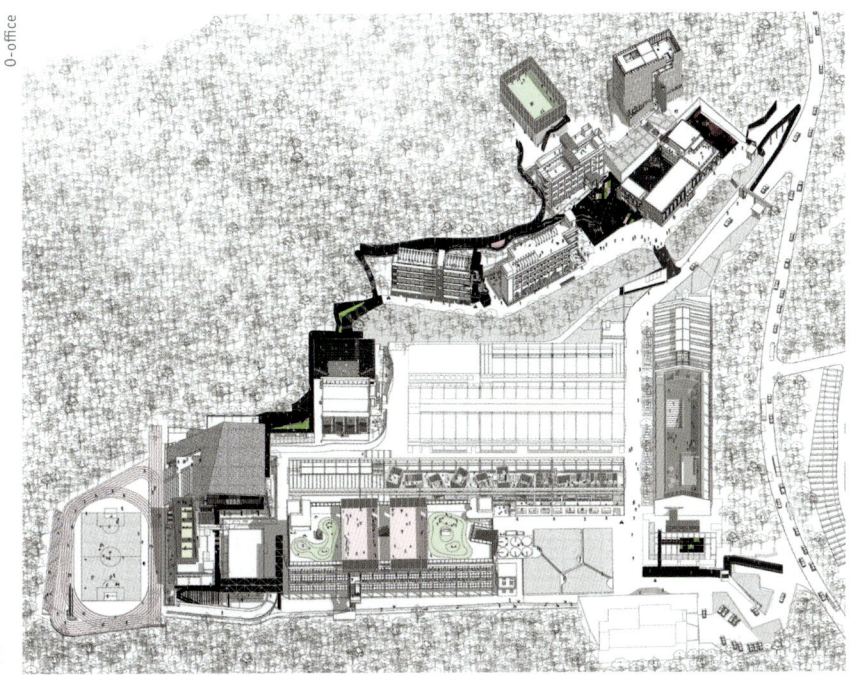

Zhang Chao

Zhang Chao

Zhang Chao

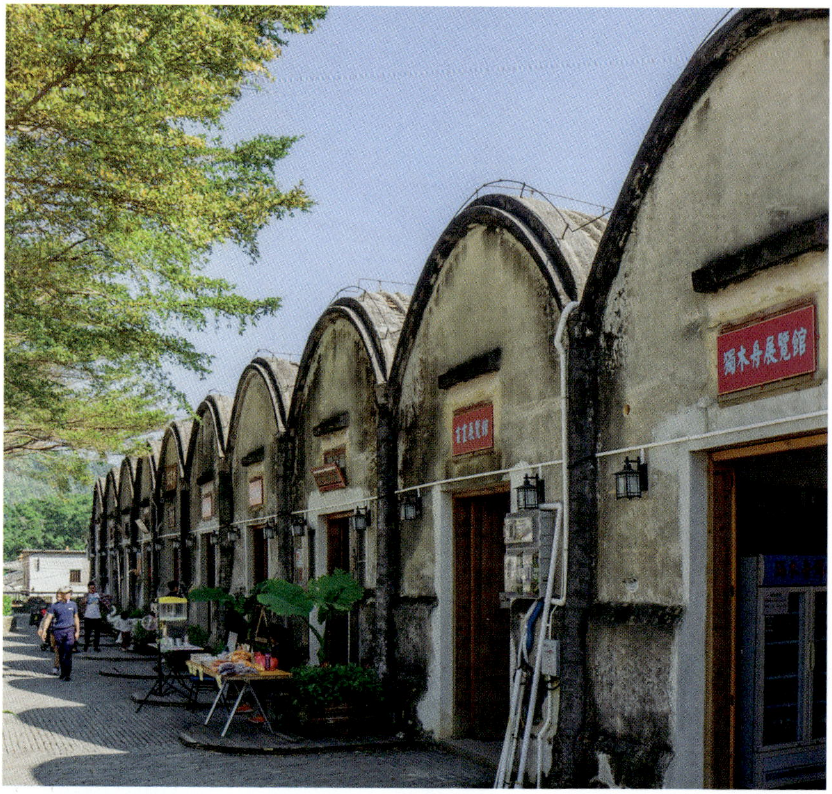

辛桂鵬

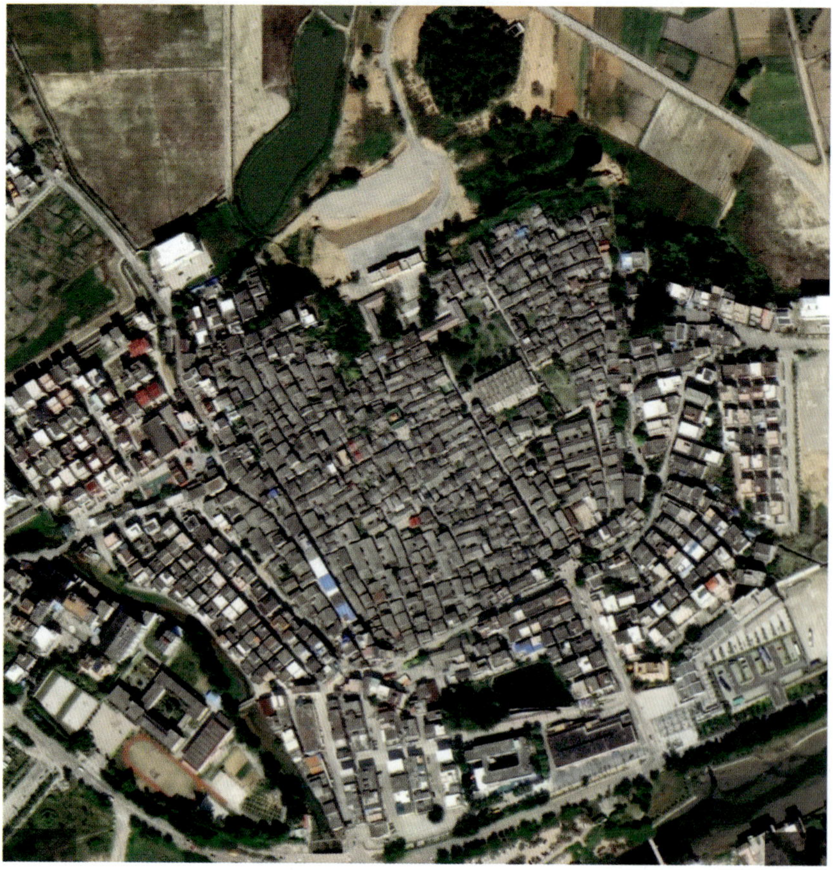

© Mapbox, © OpenStreetMap

Dapeng Fortress «

Intersection of Nanmen E Rd. &
Nanmen W Rd., Longgang
Ancient
1394

 153 J

大鹏城
龙岗区南门东路与南门西路交汇处

Line 8
Kwai Cheng Centre
葵涌中心站
15 km (Bus 818+b753)

Dapeng Village is one of the National Key
Cultural Relics that has been protected
by the State Council since 2001. The ancient fortress was built in the Ming Dynasty to resist the invasion of the pirates
and the Japanese sailing along the southern Chinese coasts. For centuries, the marine was based in Dapeng and contributed
to the flourishing of its Hakka community. Surrounded by mountains and the sea,
and oriented along the north-south axis, the walled city is still well preserved
with three main gates in the east, south,
and west. Covering an area of about
100,000 square metres, it is quite dense.
Although historical transformations have
altered the urban structure, the original
grid and the road hierarchy are still recognisable. The one- and two-storey narrow
buildings juxtapose on the narrow pedestrian streets that welcome visitors and
tourists. The village is worth the visit.

Toyama Temple
(Dongshan Temple) ⌄

Dongmen Rd., Dapeng
Ancient (Community Project)
1394 (1954)

 154 J

东山寺
大鹏区东门路

Overlooking the bay from the side of Dan
Shannan, Dongshan Temple dates back
to the same year as Dapeng Fortress. As
tradition narrates, *fengshui* master Lai
Buyi was travelling around Dapeng when,
passing near the Dongshan Dragon Stone
Mountain, he saw a purple glow, and so he
founded the temple there. Over the centuries, the temple has been rebuilt three
times: in 1854, 1993, and 2009, thanks
to the donations of locals and overseas
compatriots. The temple is divided into four main halls located in a hierarchical, scalar sequence along the mountain slope. The halls are dedicated to
Guandi's idol, Wei Tuo, Sanbao Buddha,
and the 18 Arhats. They are connected by
wide stairs, covered paths, and patios in
a linked system of continuously filtered
spaces. Since its last reconstruction, the
temple is a concrete structure building
with a clearwater stone outer wall, yellow-glazed tile eaves, and colourful decorations. An ancient stone arch is visible
near the mountain gate, with four pillars
and three beams carved out of granite.

J

Geology Museum ⌃
Geological Park Rd., Dapeng
LeeMundwiler Architects
2013

 155 J

深圳地质博物馆
龙岗区地质公园路

Line 8
Kwai Cheng Centre
葵涌中心站
19 km (Bus e11+m423)

Gaoling Hakka Village ⌄
Haijing Rd., Dapeng
Vernacular
1600s

156 J

高岭古村
大鹏区海礁路

Line 8
Kwai Cheng Centre
葵涌中心站
25.5 km (Bus e11+m274)

In the middle of the volcanic Dapeng peninsula, the Geology Museum is part of Dapeng National Park. Hidden by nature, the building unfolds gradually in front of the visitor. Its zigzag shape and stone-cladding reflect the solid matter of the mountains and evoke the tension between natural elements. The inside alternates large and narrow spaces, with dark and light atmospheres in constant mutation.

Located 200 metres above the sea level and nestled in the forest, this is a unique example of an unaltered Hakka village. Probably one of the first in the area, it was abandoned in 1992 due to its difficult location. Its buildings are decorated with a hybrid Eastern-Western style architecture, anticipating the nineteenth-century extravaganza of Kaiping style. They are still intact despite the overlying nature.

J

Buildings and Places

Sorted alphabetically with project number

Featured Architects by Project Number

Sorted alphabetically; digits indicate project numbers

Featured Architects by Page Number

Sorted alphabetically; digits indicate page numbers

'Eight years have passed. This time I come to see that Shenzhen, Zhuhai, and some other localities have undergone rapid development. It is really out of my expectations. After seeing all this, I've got enhanced confidence.'

Deng Xiaoping, 1992

Satellite view of the eastern Pearl River Delta, 1978

'We built our first project here in Shenzhen, a park design, and it was demolished after two years. It was not supposed to be temporary and we spent huge amounts of energy and effort to make it work in the best way...Then suddenly they demolished it and they built something new on it; they really deceived us. That's the speed!'

Liu Xiaodu, URBANUS

Satellite view, 2001

'The speed at which Shenzhen is recreating itself makes it difficult to remember what the city has been.'

Mary Ann O'Donnell

Satellite view, 2020

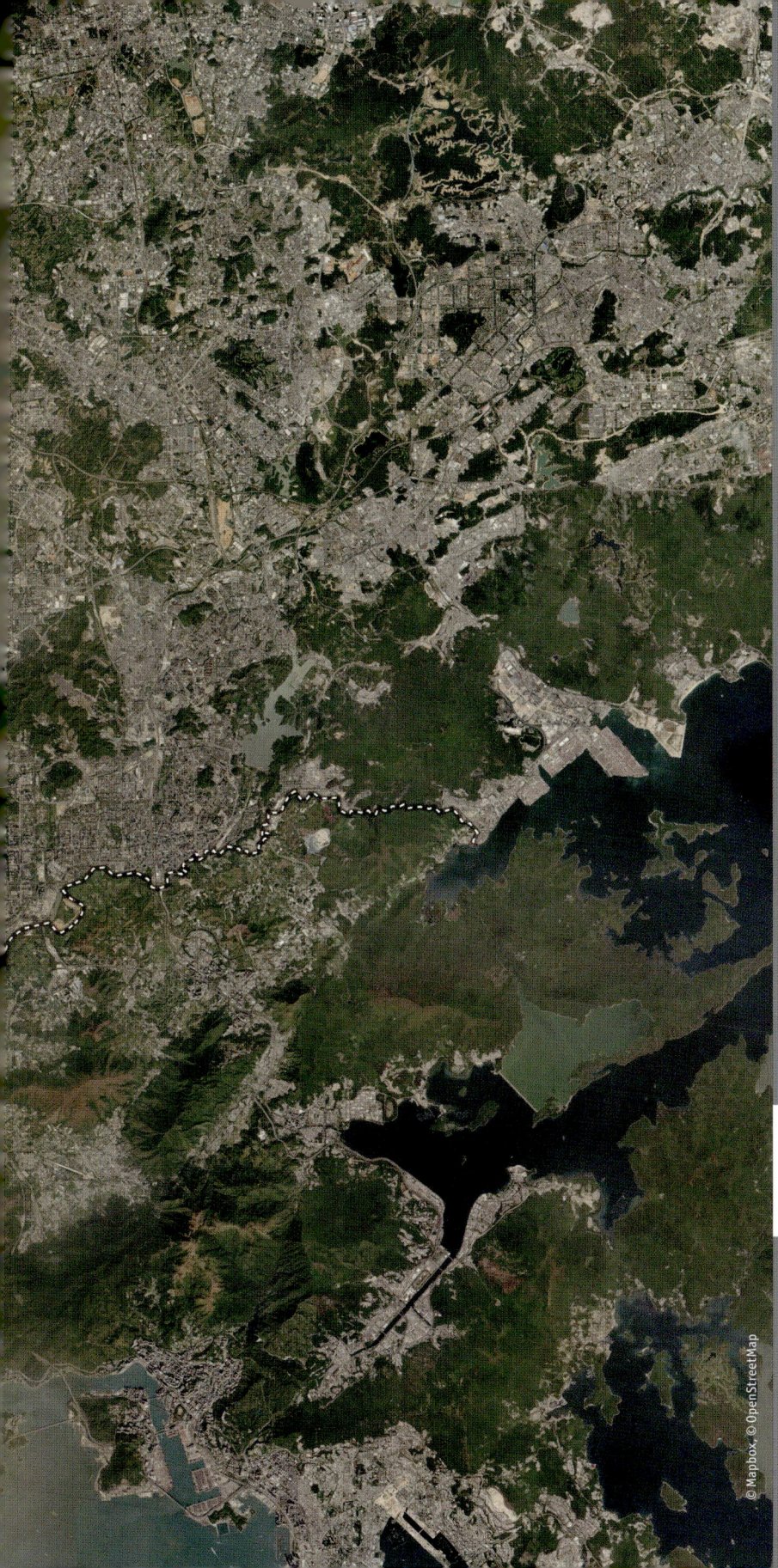

© Mapbox, © OpenStreetMap

A view of Shennan Road and the Deng Xiaoping Billboard from Diwang Tower (see p. 58)

Acknowledgements

This book is the outgrowth of nearly 12 years spent researching Shenzhen architectural and urban history. Since the first visit as an exchange student at Shenzhen University followed by a series of research trips, several encounters with local colleagues, architects, and scholars have helped me outline a unique sense of belonging with this city.

Firstly, sincere thanks to the publisher Philipp Meuser and publishing director Björn Rosen of DOM publishers for having believed in me to make Shenzhen part of the Architectural Guide series. Loving thanks to my husband Giuseppe, who motivated me to work on this book during the COVID-19 pandemic lockdowns and during all of the hard times over the last year. Special thanks to my parents, who supported my continuous desire to dedicate my energy to architecture first and then to Chinese studies. Sincere thanks to professors Cristina Pallini, Maurizio Meriggi, Vincenzo Donato, Federico Acuto, and Chen Zhen, who encouraged my early interest in the Chinese urban phenomena during my studies at Polytechnic of Milan, and to Lucia Nucci, my PhD tutor at the Third University of Rome, who helped me evolve my critical thinking on Shenzhen and the cultural implications behind its development. Late thanks to Marcus Lloyd Andresen, a mentor who believed in me and trained me to love the visual poetry of the built environment and its details. Profound thanks to Xing Guipeng (辛桂鹏), a rising photographer from Shenzhen who contributed to this book with tons of impressive photographs; we shared many emails full of thoughts on photography and the city's history over the last year, and I consider him a good friend.

Finally, I would like to thank all the architectural firms, photographers, and institutions for their kind provision of images for this book. In particular, I want to thank the individual staff members who handled my inquiries with attentive consideration: Arch-Exist, Aether Architects, Arata Isozaki & Associates, Bjarke Ingels Group, BLACKhome, Coop Himmelb(l)au, Christoph Monschein, DO Architects, EDAW- AECOM, gmp Architekten, Georges Hung, Gravity Partnership, Guan Shanming Architects, Hans Hollein, Ingame, Maki and Associates, Massimiliano and Doriana Fuksas, Mecanoo, MLA+, Mozhao Architects, OMA, O-office, OPEN Architecture, PleasantHouse Design, Rocco Design Architects Associates, SHUISHI, Skidmore, Owings & Merrill, Steven Holl Architects, Studio Link-Arc, Studio Pei-Zhu, Tate Snyder Kimsey Architects, URBANUS, XING Guipeng, and Wutopia Lab.

Image Credits

Incense coils in Guandi Temple (see p. 147)

Author

Domenica Bona, PhD

Domenica Bona (1986) is an Italian PhD architect with variegated experience in design and research, from architecture, to urban planning, to editorial and media. Domenica holds an M.Arch from Polytechnic of Milan School of Civil Architecture and a PhD from the Third University of Rome. Recognised with the INU Award 2018, her doctoral thesis investigates the concept of 'Chinese-ness' in contemporary Chinese cities' images through the application of a morphological approach. In 2010, she moved to China to study architecture and urban design at Shenzhen University, where she developed her deep interest in the urban morphology and architectural history of China and Far East Asia. Since then, a yearly series of research trips around the country have allowed her to visit the most remote villages and participate in several research seminars in Beijing, Xiamen, and Wuhan universities, among other institutions.

Focused on architectural design and branding in practice, Domenica is also a founding member of RebelArchitette, an association that promotes equity in the architectural profession internationally. She remains active in academia in Italy and abroad and she is currently a lecturer at the China Centre of the Technical University of Berlin, where she leads a course on architecture and cities in modern and contemporary China across cultures, styles, and gender issues.

The *Deutsche Nationalbibliothek* lists this publication in the *Deutsche Nationalbibliografie;*
detailed bibliographic data are available at
http://dnb.d-nb.de.

ISBN 978-3-86922-265-3

© 2022 by DOM publishers, Berlin
www.dom-publishers.com

Proofreading
Grace Pettey

Layout
Domenica Bona

Final artwork
Nicole Wolf

QR-Codes
Christoph Gößmann

Printing
Bilnet Matbaacılık ve Yayıncılık A. Ş., Istanbul
www.bilnet.net.tr